THE ART OF PSYCHOLOGICAL MANIPULATION

Life-Changing Techniques to discover how to manipulate people with Dark Psychology secrets, Persuasion, Mind Control, Body Language Analysis, Hypnosis, and NLP.

By

ROBERT REED

Table Of Contents

book has been derived from various sources. Please consult a licensed professional before attempting any techniques outlined in this book.

By reading this document, the reader agrees that under no circumstances is the author responsible for any losses, direct or indirect, that are incurred as a result of the use of the information contained within this document, including, but not limited to errors, omissions, or inaccuracies.

YOUR FREE GIFT

As a way of saying thank you for your purchase, I'm offering you a premium content which will help you discover many common mistakes in early face-to-face meetings, both business and private, and boost your self-awareness and your confidence.

Just search this site on your favorite browser: **https://mailchi.mp/8c5af94283ef/theartofpsychologicalmanipulation** and you will receive all the contents for free, in a comfortable printable PDF format!

Visit the official website: www.robert-reed.org for the latest news in terms of personal improvement, to receive new content always updated, videos, stay informed about training events organized throughout the country, and much more!

DOWNLOAD THE AUDIO VERSION OF THIS BOOK FOR FREE

If you love listening to audiobook on-the-go or would you enjoy a narration as you read along, I have great news for you. You can download the audiobook version of *The Art of Psychological Manipulation* for FREE just by signing up for a FREE 30-days Audible trial!

Introduction

Human relationships, at all levels, are critical to all life endeavors. You need the acceptance and commitment of people to achieve your dreams and aspirations in life. However, many do not know how to go about it. In the bid to win over others, some become vulnerable and become victims of people with hidden agendas. It can be frustrating when you know something is wrong but have no idea how to fix it. Making relationships work can be challenging without quality information on how to succeed in them.

At a point in my life, I had terrible interpersonal and working relationships. My communication skills were not impressive, and this affected my interpersonal and professional relationships. I had a job as a sales representative in a company, and sales were low due to my inability to convince prospective buyers. In hindsight, I am glad that I was objective enough to discern that something was missing. I will be sharing the tips that transformed my life with you in this book.

Many individuals in the world today, in all spheres of life, lack excellent communication skills. Meanwhile, significant interactions are the fulcrum of successful interpersonal and professional relationships. If you are a parent with rebellious kids or an entrepreneur struggling to inspire your team members, this book is for you.

By training, I am a psychologist that specializes in ADV. I have had a series of experiences in my past and my present that made me delve into human behaviors. Currently, I am committed to helping and counseling people who have the same problem I had to help them get over it. For instance, last year, a young man came into my office, seeking my guidance. He didn't want to attend the university his parents recommended for him. He needed me to give him the right approach to communicate his decision to them amicably. Through some of the steps that will be discussed in this book, he convinced them.

Also, from my experience, I got to know that many people manipulate their audience, customers, children, and other people to do what they want. My knowledge as a human behaviorist has exposed me to the two types of manipulation: white and dark. Most times, white manipulation is without psychological violence; but dark manipulation is orchestrated with psychological violence. Psychological violence includes lies, guilt, fear, etc.

In this book, you will learn the best techniques and benefits of a robust relationship with your audience. You will understand the foundations of creating excellent relationships and how to sustain them to your advantage. Moreover, you will find easy guidelines that, if followed, will improve your engagement and will want others to listen to your ideas. Note that your success in life depends on the opportunities you get. So, possessing skills that will pave the way for more approvals of your ideas will improve the quality of your life.

You would be shown why people want the latest Apple products and rely heavily on Microsoft. Besides, you will also understand how Mary Kay convinced ladies to patronize its products. This book will teach you how to understand body language and use it for your benefit. Also, you will be taught why others decline most of your views, and how you can change their perspective. Indeed, this is a complete guide that will improve your relationships in all ramifications.

Regardless of the area of life, you will find tips that can help you to up your game. You will learn from fantastic examples that captivate their target audience with their ability to use words decisively. Their methods and approach to interpersonal and professional relationships will serve as a blueprint for your success.

This book will take you chapter by chapter in the simplest ways to enhance your ability to influence people. It will also give you inklings on how to get your kid's respect and appreciation. You have picked up the right material if you want to persuade your customers to invest in your products consistently. Anyone can be an entrepreneur. However, it takes skills and grit to succeed in your endeavor. Excellent customer relationships and services are an integral part of your success.

More so, reading this book will broaden your horizons on manipulation. You will know how to identify manipulators, when you are being manipulated, and how to get out of a manipulative relationship. This book focuses on dark manipulation, which is psychological violence. It explains hypnosis and dark psychology, which are the tools of dark manipulation. How they work, can be done, and protect yourself from them will also be extensively discussed.

If you pay attention while reading, you will find exciting and enlightening tips you apply in your relationships. This material can be life-changing, depending on your attitude to it. It has laid down guidelines that can transform your relationships in months of careful practice and adherence. So, you must study intending of getting the best out of it. In no time, you can find yourself as the center of attention. You can become a source of inspiration to your family member, friends, spouse, and colleagues. It all depends on your attitude. The journey begins!

CHAPTER ONE

Persuasion Skill From Advertising World

Many talented individuals are not able to use their prowess to the fullest because they lacked the one necessary ingredient: persuasion. Many relationships have crumbled, opportunities missed, sales not made, and customers lost because of inappropriate approaches to human interactions.

W. Clement Stones was given birth to a very low-income family, and his father died, leaving debts behind. He had to sell Newspapers on the south side of Chicago. After some time, he got fed up with hawking on the streets, and he started selling his newspaper at restaurants. Initially, the managers of the restaurants disagreed with his style, but soon, he was able to convince them that the customers didn't have a problem with it. He won them over through his charm, persistence, and politeness, and this is a short story of the growth of his success in the insurance business.

In his words, "Sales are contingent upon the attitude of the salesman – not the attitude of the prospect." This simply means that if you want to get the right response from others, it is up to you to persuade them. Your approach can go a long way in convincing even the staunchest pessimist. This chapter explores how you can leverage the persuasion skills of top brands in the modern world to improve the quality of your life.

Brand Or Quality?

Customer behavior is an exciting discussion in psychology. Studies have proven that most people buy products because of the brand rather than because of their quality. You may not realize the influence of the psychological games top companies play with your mind. When they have successfully done their magic on you, you will associate quality with a brand name. Once this happens, you will stop evaluating the company's products objectively. You will be convinced that every of its product is top quality.

It gets so bad that you will buy a more expensive product from a famous brand rather than a cheaper one from another company. Interestingly, the less expensive product might be better than the pricey one. Nonetheless, because the renowned brand has won your heart, you will not mind the cost of the product. This psychological influence accounts for the monopoly of many reputable brands in a particular sector.

In the modern world, thriving brands are always keen to make improvements that keep them relevant. These companies find ways to persuade you to buy their products psychologically. For instance, Nike endorses sports celebrities to market their products. The company leverages the fame of the likes of Neymar Junior, a famous footballer, to persuade prospective buyers to patronize its products. This strategy has made Nike one of the wealthiest footwear companies in the world. This is a far cry from the 1980s when the company was just a casual shoe firm. However, things are different today because they changed their approach.

Know Their Wants

Walt Disney, at an early age, was sent packing because he was said not to be creative. He later became the owner of the most significant animation industry. He found out that many kids wanted to wander into the fantasy world, and he met their needs by creating a series of animated characters that the kids later got to love. To engage your target audience, you must know their wants and find a way to satisfy their desires.

Prospective clients will be willing to venture into business with you if you can show them that they will benefit from you in the long run. For instance, the insurance companies show you that if you give them a certain amount of your money annually, you will be secured if anything happens to your insured. They will tell you that they will replace your car or repair it at no additional cost if you guarantee it with them with a certain amount of money. Also, they have the life policies, which make the family of those insured to get a premium sum of money after the death of the insurer.

You cannot succeed in convincing people when you do not know what they desire. So, the first step when presenting ideas to others is to know what they want. For instance, most phone companies don't just say they've developed a new phone; they make people know that their new phones have some new features that would benefit their clients.

More so, most brands add new features to their phones every year to get customers to crave their products. These additions range from security features such as keyboard unlock to fingerprint sensor unlock and recently, face unlock. These phones bring new and convenient features that make previous products look outdated. I had a friend in college that changed his phone every year. There was a time I asked him why he changed his phone every year, and he told me that the phone companies add new features to the phone that makes his files safer and easier to access.

These phone companies understand that humans like to use new things. They know that most people want the satisfaction of being a part of a new trend. So, these brands work tirelessly to develop new exciting features to make their customers invest in the latest products. In the same way, you need to know what the people in your life want. If you understand the desires of your spouse, you will get along well. Also, if you know the expectations of your boss, it will be easier to meet them.

Satisfy The Demands

Knowing what the people in your life want is a fantastic start. Nonetheless, it is not good enough to keep their attention. You need to be able to devise practical strategies to meet the needs. This strategy is the secret of top firms. They leverage several means such as online surveys and other customer feedback platforms, to know their clients' demands. Once they get these responses, they set out to make changes or create products to enhance customer satisfaction.

In 2007, Apple released its first iPhone under glass, and in 2009, the company became well known in the whole world when they released their products into the major markets in the world. How? Before they released their phones, various products were already circulating in the market, including flip-flops, slides, etc. However, they knew that their target market wanted better network connection, improved screen touch setups, enhanced cameras, just to mention a few.

So, they incorporated these features into their phones, and many customers went for their products. Now, Apple is one of the biggest and richest companies globally, with nothing less than seven hundred and fifty-three billion dollars in assets. Besides, it has more than two hundred and three million dollars in cash.

You can take a cue from this company's approach. Before you can have someone listen to you, you must first realize their wants and think about the best way to satisfy them. Whenever you are talking, they will find you more exciting and worth their time. No one wants to engage a person who just keeps talking about things that do not pique their interest. Therefore, in your relationships and business, it is critical to identify needs and meet them.

Seek Creative Ways To Meet Demands

Making plans to meet demands is good. Nonetheless, you need to go beyond that. Many of us have what it takes to get that respect, to get that promotion, to make that sale, to keep that relationship, but what we don't have is the ability to sway the people to see our view and how it can benefit them. You must be ready to do more than the norm to achieve remarkable results. You need to avoid getting yourself involved in meaningless activities. Take out time to think about better ways to do things that can sell you to your target audience.

In the early 1900s, Milwaukee Schlitz, a beer brewer ranked eighth in America, suddenly rose to number one. What happened? He hired Claude Hopkins, one of the founding fathers of modern advertising, to advertise his products to gain more customers. Hopkins didn't understand the beer product and the market, so Schlitz had to give him a tour. All beer brewers at that time always talked about how clean and pure their product is without actually showing anyone how they did it.

As Schlitz was taking Hopkins through his company, through the equipment and its usage, he found out that Schlitz sterilized all his beer bottles at least four times before use. He also noticed that Schlitz gets water from four thousand foot-deep artesian wells. Besides, Schlitz did over one 1002 experiments to produce yeast cells for brewing. Hopkins was fascinated by all these and asked Schlitz why he didn't tell people what he did to brew beer. His answer? "All brewers do the same thing."

The media expert advised him to create awareness. Meanwhile, it was something other brewers had never thought of doing. Hopkins made an advert which stipulated, "Ask your doctor about Schlitz beer. He knows the importance of purity. Tell him that Schlitz beer is aged for months before it is marketed. He will say it cannot cause biliousness. Tell him that every bottle is purified after it is sealed. He will say that such a beer must be germless. Ask your doctor what these virtues mean to you."

After the release of this advert, in a couple of months, Schlitz beer came from number eight to number one. Hopkins knew what people wanted; they wanted to know that the beers they take are pure and wouldn't affect them, and that was what he gave them. In your professional and interpersonal relationships, you need to apply this principle of creativity in meeting demands. For example, don't just accuse your boss of favoring other people in the organization.

What you see as favoritism might be a meritocracy. In other words, your employee might be promoting others and raising their pay because they offer more to the company's collective course than you. Therefore, you need to be objective in your analysis. Do you go the extra mile to ensure that you get the job done? What have you done during the periods you were allowed to show what you can do? A different approach can turn things around for you.

Do Not Quit

Note that it takes time to make people accept your view. Everyone is persuadable; however, it requires the right timing and context. For instance, in 2008, during the election campaign, I have a friend that always said he would never vote for Barack Obama. We closely watched the campaign of both candidates, and at the final round, my friend was swayed by his speech.

My friend abhorred Barack Obama's candidacy for the White House initially. However, after a series of campaigns, he started getting swayed by the brilliance of the man. There was a time he defended his view on foreign policy even though he was still adamant that he would never vote for him. He was getting to like him over time and was won over eventually.

What I want to bring out in the example above is that Barack Obama didn't sway my friend into voting for him in a night; it was a gradual process. If your first approach towards getting your kids to respect and appreciate you, getting the promotion, making the sale goes awry, do not give up. With time, you can still be able to achieve your goals. You lose the opportunity to make the right impression when you stop trying.

It can be frustrating to wait, but it is often worth it if you refuse to lose hope in your dreams. Abraham Lincoln was the sixteenth president of the United States of American (1861-1865). He didn't become the president of the US on his first trial, but through persistence and creating awareness.

When I was working at a store for my upkeep in college, the manager never saw why to give me a raise when I first asked for it. He even threatened to fire me if I continued to ask him. However, I was not deterred. I buckled down and showed by worth. I stayed for more hours, did more chores, and at the end of the month, he gave me a raise. The beginning might be challenging; however, if you persist, in no time, you will be able to sway those people that have been turning deaf ears to your views. You will make those sales, get that promotion, your kids will appreciate you, and your parents will listen to you.

CHAPTER TWO

Why People Say 'No'

Most times, being rejected does not mean you don't know what you are saying or that your products are low-grade. Indeed, some people may not buy your products because they don't need those items by then. Nonetheless, excellent persuasion skills can make customers buy products even when they don't need them. If you think about it, you will realize that you have invested in products that are of no use to you because the seller was too engaging. You can have that kind of influence on the people around you.

You may have the right ideas, but still, lose a business deal to a better presenter. Have you ever wondered why the man with a product gets his products accepted and you with the good one get declined? Bad advice gets accepted, and your useful pieces of advice get rejected? It all has to do with how they showcased themselves in the most appealing way to their audience. This chapter will review the reasons you get turned down and how you can turn the table around.

Saying The Right Thing At The Right Time

One of the questions that bothered my mind is, "Why do people say 'no'?" Previously, while talking to a person, I often know what I am talking about, and it would seem to be the best for me at the moment. However, at the end of our discussion, I still get turned down. I thought I was alone but soon realized that many people are suffering from the same thing. We have good ideas, but we can't say them in captivating ways, which later make us get declined or rejected.

I realized that saying the right things is not enough; I must say them at the right time. Besides, I must also know my audience before speaking. If I present the right ideas to the wrong people, my effort will be futile. For example, if you sell luxurious and pricey shoes, targeting middle-class earners is a waste of time. You need to appeal to the high-class prospective clients who can afford such items.

The mood of the listener also goes a long way in determining the response you get. Your spouse may reject an idea not because it is silly, but because he or she is stressed. So, you should avoid talking to people when they are not happy or exhausted. You might say the right things during these periods, but timing will frustrate your effort. Always wait for the right time to push your ideas home to increase your chances of getting approvals.

Approaches That Can Lead To Rejection

There are certain things you say either consciously or subconsciously that can get you a rejection. This means there are ways you can talk that can make your audience uncertain about what you are saying. Meanwhile, once doubts set in their hearts, they will not want to buy your idea. The following tips will help you gain the trust of others:

Sound Confident

One of the things that get you a no from people is that you don't sound confident. When you are uncertain in your presentation, whatever they say can never be accepted. Everyone wants to be sure that you are not wasting their time. Your kids want to know that you are instructing them because you are sure of the outcome. Similarly, your spouse wants to be guaranteed that the new approach will not harm your kids. Your boss wants to be sure that your business idea will not lead to financial loss for the company.

A mode of speech that will unequivocally get you a no is when you talk, but you don't give straightforward statements. For instance, if customers visit your store, they want to be guaranteed that you are selling superior quality products. If the person asks you about the effectiveness of the product, your response should express confidence.

Failure to do so will make the client look for somewhere else that offers assurance.

A patient wants to be sure that he or she gets treated by the right doctor. If he or she asks, "Is the doctor an expert?" The last thing he or she wants to hear is a nurse saying, "Well, I don't know, but you are safe." The patient would most definitely decline to go into the theatre with a doctor he/she doesn't think is capable enough. Also, if a lawyer needs to defend the life of his client, and the client asks, "Are you well prepared for this matter?" and the lawyer replies with, "Not really, but we will be alright." The "Not really" would send an alarm to the brains of the client, and he would want to get another lawyer to defend him. The same applies to persuasion. You can never persuade someone if you do not offer certainty.

Do Your Homework

An integral factor that will build your confidence when speaking is making the necessary findings beforehand. For example, if you are a sales representative, you should have a good grasp of the pros and cons of the company's products. Failure to do so will make it difficult to assure customers that they will get value for their money by investing in a product.

Whenever you are uncertain, people wouldn't take you seriously. Moreover, if they don't, they would most certainly decline any proposals you have for them, regardless of how juicy it is. So, to avoid sounding like you are not sure, ask the right questions beforehand. Think about the likely questions you might be asked and provide the correct answers to them. Never present an idea that has obvious loopholes.

Before speaking to your kids, think about the questions they might ask you. When you don't sound logical, they may not argue with you out of respect but will not do your biddings. Similarly, before presenting a business idea to prospective investors, think about what they may want to know and be ready to provide a logical answer.

Avoid Weasel Words

There is something called weasel words, and they are often used in statements. However, if you want to persuade someone to do something for you, you must stop using these words. Many weasel words will turn people completely off from what you are saying regardless of how detailed you may seem to be. If you want to persuade people to do what you want, you must desist from using them.

"**Probably/Possibly**" are examples of weasel words. These words are subconsciously used when you are not sure about a product. For instance, if you want to get a promotion, and your boss asks, "Are you going to be able to handle the stress?" Replying with "probably" inputs in his or her mind that you cannot handle the role. That response implies that you are not fit for the position.

A phrase like "**Could be**" can also be problematic. It makes you sound uninformed, and you cannot make anyone do your biddings if you don't have enough information. It could be detrimental if used when trying to explain how and why something works the way it does. For instance, if a customer asks, "what does this product do?" Your response should not be, "It could be it is used for making toast." Immediately, the customer would know you know nothing about what you are trying to sell to him or her.

Starting a statement with "**Well**" is also a bad habit. It would never make you sound sure of yourself to whomever you are trying to persuade. If someone asks you a question, and you start with "well," it makes you sound doubtful, and no one is easily convinced by a person that says uncertainly. If you are asked a question, give a straightforward answer.

Use Case Studies

It is easier to convince someone about an idea or product when you have specific examples of beneficiaries. Using words like "**some**" or "**many**" while trying to convince someone will do more harm than good. These words don't add much legitimacy to your statement. It seems more like you are speculating, which will make the person listening to doubt you.

For instance, you should not tell your son, "Some kids your age are doing this effectively." Instead, you should say, "Greg did this last week and was able to do it effectively." He knows Greg and can easily copy that template. A lawyer, when making a citation, can never say, "in some cases..." he would always say "in the case of X v Y."

This is also useful information for those that are into business and want more clients. If you are speculative, there is a high possibility that your product would not be bought. If a customer asks how products have been used, and you say, "Some of our customers have used it, and it has worked effectively for them." This would never sway them to buy your product. However, if you say, "Mrs. Ryan, that I worked with several months ago, bought this product, and it worked effectively for her." This makes you more assertive to sway the customers easily because you have given them a person who used it.

Things You Write That Gets You A "No."

It is not every time that you have to present an idea with your voice; you might find yourself in situations where you will have to use your words in writing to convince others. Most people don't have the unique skill set required to persuade people using written words. The following tips will help you win your audience over when writing to them:

Keep The Readers In Mind

There are various mistakes made when writing that prevents you from getting the right response. These errors can make your well-written work watery. The first mistake you make when writing is that you don't have your audience in mind. Beautiful writing is one thing; passing the message across to the requisite audience is another. Most writers are fluent but don't the results their ostensibly fantastic write-ups deserve.

What you need for you to have an endearing write-up is for you to know your audience. Understand their world view, current challenges, and how you can reinforce or change their belief system.

Steve Harvey, the writer of *'Think Like a Man,"* excelled because he knew his audience. I identified them as ladies who had suffered or didn't want to suffer emotionally in the hand of men.

He wrote a book that would solve their problems by explaining to them how the man thinks, what his beliefs were, and how he behaved to women. He explained the reaction women would get from men if they act in a manner. Moreover, the author persuaded its target audience to buy the book, read it, and make use of the information.

That is where the difference lies between a write-up that would persuade and one that would not. Once a writer fails to understand the peculiarities of his or her target audience, failure is inevitable. Many ideas that could have been blockbusters today never took off because they were presented to the wrong people. As an entrepreneur, do your research about the target market to offer them a cutting-edge product. Little tweaks like this can change your fortunes tremendously.

Provide Details As Much As Possible

There was this one time I was reading a newspaper, and I saw an advert on a gum. What was in the advert was "Buy our product; it is one of the best." I immediately flipped the page of the paper because I was disgusted by the advert. Why is it the best? Why should I buy it? These were the questions that were going on in my mind. The advertiser failed woefully to persuade me to opt for his gum because the advert was not well written.

Steve Harvey is a sterling example of how detailing when writing can make a whole lot of difference. He knew that he was writing the book for women, and his main focus was to show them the depths of how a man thinks. That was what he needed to know and work on, which made the book the best seller. Women who had been dumped for no reason, who had been deceived, and manipulated by men, were all discussed in the book.

Just like this author, you need to provide details when writing. It is not good enough to just make blatant statements. You should give explanations as much as possible. That gum company should have cited the selling points that make its product superior to conventional ones. Never forget that you will not be there when the reader is going through the texts. So, offer them useful details that will hammer home your points.

Mind Your Tone

You should also know that when you are writing, you should take cognizance of your tone. You may be able to identify your target audience. However, the wrong style can still make your presentation repulsive. For instance, if you are writing for a law magazine, you have to be formal in your tone. However, if you do the same when writing entertainment stories, it will be counterproductive.

The way you write a children's column is not the same way you write an article for adults. An article that will be read by kids must be filled with simple words and broken into shorter paragraphs. Meanwhile, it is acceptable to use complicated words, especially when writing to adults who are experts in a particular field.

You cannot be writing to tech enthusiasts without using terms that are peculiar to that aspect. Most people will drop the article after reading two paragraphs. In a highly-competitive world, you need to be at your best in your endeavors. It becomes vital to be concise and precise when posting on an online platform. There are several similar articles available to the readers. So, you cannot afford to get your tone wrong.

Avoid Fallacies

Another reason why most people cannot persuade others to agree with their views is that they base their writing on faulty logic. What do I mean? Many writers use straw man arguments, which don't add up if it is carefully examined. For instance, Steve Harvey didn't use faulty logic while writing, "Think like a Man." He researched most men and how they behave towards women before he wrote his books. He gave a series of examples in the book with credible references. So, it is not shocking that the book gained popularity and became a US bestseller.

If you are willing to gain the attention of your audience through your writings, you must be able to guide them towards a common realization through the use of logically sound and credible arguments. You must have researched the topic before you write it down. If you stick to fallacies, your integrity and credibility as a writer would be tainted, and you will not be able to convince your readers.

For example, you might want to pitch a business theory at your workplace and want the boards of directors to approve it. Not only what you have said in your presentation would sway them into agreeing with you, but they will also read the report on the idea you have submitted to them. If your presentation was top-notch, but your report is watery and filled with fallacies, it would most definitely be rejected.

Avoid Writing In The Negative

There are various things you add to your writings that would never make you persuade your audience. You might not think of those things as big deals. However, they go a long way in dissuading your audience about your views. One of the things that turn people off from your writing is when you write in the negative. Many writers might not know that their mode of writing is in the negative.

Your first paragraph can be enough to turn the audience off. If you want to write and persuade people, your thesis must be stated in the first paragraph. They often turn the readers off by saying things that make them mad. Your write-ups might be interesting, amusing, or great. However, it will not make the desired impact if you use words that are disgusting and awful. You will never be able to sway your readers if your words are repulsive and unpleasant.

Imagine that Steve Harvey started his first paragraph with "women are stupid, that is the reason why men treat them like trash." What would come into your mind as a woman if you read such a paragraph? You would instantly feel insulted, and his book would not be appealing to you again. Meanwhile, it might contain life-transforming ideas in the subsequent pages.

A few years ago, a colleague of mine with low self-esteem wrote at the beginning of his work, "It is not a great idea, but it could just work." Our supervisors didn't even bother to read his work. Why? He simply stated at the beginning that they would just stress themselves if they read the piece.

Don't Use Threatening Words

Another thing that would always repel your readers is if you threaten them. This has never been an excellent way to win someone over to your side. Threats would work against what you aim to achieve. For instance, you wrote a letter for a promotion, and you put in the message, "if I don't get this promotion, I am quitting." Sometimes, this works, but most times, it works against the writer.

It is unimaginable for a lawyer to threaten the judge in his written address or submission. Imagine, he writes, "If you don't acquit my client, will you lose your job?" The lawyer's case would get struck out, or the lawyer finds himself in jail for contempt. Using threatening language or tone in your writing could annoy the readers, and your aim would be dashed.

Avoid Bandwagon Persuasion

Using bandwagon persuasion is another form of influence that might be fruitless. What is Bandwagon persuasion? Simply, it means trying to convince your readers to approve an idea because most people are doing it. Meanwhile, some people believe that they are unique and don't get swayed because most are doing it. For instance, if you want to persuade your boss for a raise, your reason should not be because a rival company did the same. Sometimes, it could work, and you will be able to persuade your audience; however, most times, it would work against you.

Instead of telling your boss to give you a raise because a rival company is doing it, ask him to do because you deserve it. Produce facts on what you have done to get for salary increment. In the same way, it is not proper to tell your spouse to buy you a gift because others are doing it. Such comparison can be repulsive and make your partner discouraged.

There was a time I wanted my parents to buy me a car. My Dad asked me why I wanted a car, and my answer was, "because most of my friends are using cars." My Dad looked at me scornfully and never talked about the issue again until two years later. I shouldn't have used a bandwagon persuasion on my Dad; I should have shown him that I spend too much money taking a bus and taxi home.

Don't Be Ambiguous

You should never use a vague tone when you are trying to persuade people in your writing. They might interpret it wrongly. You should know that what is good or bad is subjective. If something good for you, it might be wrong in the view of others. So, if you put such ambiguity in your work, it may work against you. In your writing, you should be very straightforward with your audience.

For instance, at the beginning of your write-up, you should develop something like "Life is Beautiful." This is vague without explanations. You might be saying that because of your upbringing. You might never have lived through revolutions, death, and war. However, if your target audience is some people from African countries facing conflict, poverty, and diseases, they may not see things in the same light. It is better to say, "Life is beautiful when you focus on the positive aspects."

Why Not Being Empathetic Gets You A "No"

Also, another primary reason why people don't get persuaded by you is that you are not empathetic enough in what you are saying. Empathy is the awareness of the feelings and the emotions of others. You need to put yourself in the shoes of your audience to present a message that resonates with their condition.

In the words of Daniel Goleman, empathy is the ability to understand others' emotions. If you want to get more favorable responses, you must be empathetic towards the person. For example, if you're going to encourage a customer to buy your product, you must consider the way the person will feel about what you are saying. If you were in the person's situation, will you buy the product based on the recommendations of a sales agent like you?

According to Daniel Goleman, there are many critical elements of empathy that makes others do your biddings. They are: Understanding others, developing others, having a service orientation, leveraging diversity, just to mention a few. The first element is critical to your objective of successfully convincing someone to agree with you. You can never persuade someone you don't understand. You must sense people's feelings and perspectives to take an active interest in their concerns.

Your listener wants to see genuine affection. He or she wants to know that you are not encouraging them to decide for your selfish interest. It can be tricky to do this if you are representing a firm. Nonetheless, if you seek to offer value to your clients while increasing your company's sales, it must be evident to the customers that you want to improve their lives.

The World Does Not Revolve Around You

Talking about empathy, I remember one of my younger sister's birthday. She had pestered me to take her to the cinema to watch a movie that was trending amongst her friends. I concurred, and I took her to the cinema. On getting to the cinema, I saw a better movie, and I wanted us to watch it. She refused flatly, and we went our separate ways; she went for the movie we initially came to watch, and I went to for the one I felt was the better movie. After the incident at the cinema, she didn't agree with anything I said. I was labeled inconsiderate and insensitive.

I could have easily watched the other movie some other time, but I refused to feel her need to have her big brother around her on her birthday. What I am trying to bring out from this example is that I wasn't considerate. I should have realized that the world does not revolve around me. After all, it was her birthday and not mine. I lost the opportunity to get her to do other things that day because I was selfish.

You can also empathize with people by acting on their needs and concerns. Political figures adopt this particular element in their bid to persuade people to vote them into office. Why did Barack Obama win the election in 2008? His approach was to make people's lives better, better work-life, more robust military, etc. He convinced Americans because he made them believe that he would focus on their needs and concerns.

Have A Service Orientation

If what you are saying to someone doesn't have to do with you developing them in any way, you would find it difficult to persuade them. Empathy can also be demonstrated by showing people that you have a service orientation. Having a service orientation means putting the needs of others into consideration. Most people don't have this orientation, and it is one of the reasons why they find it difficult to sway others.

For example, if you walk into a drug store to buy aspirin, and the attendant gave you a very unwelcoming gesture, would you like to go back to the place? No. It is evident that he lacked service orientation and has dissuaded you from going to the store again. Perhaps, when you were about to leave, the attendant tried to intimate you on a new thing to buy. You are most certainly going to decline because when you entered, he did not treat you well. It applies to everyone; if you don't demonstrate the desire to put the needs of others first, they would never give you a favorable response.

Leverage Diversity

Another way you can be empathetic is when you leverage diversity. This simply means that you tailor the way you interact with others to fit their needs and feelings. Remember that people are not the same, and you need to appreciate individual differences in your dealings. It doesn't mean that you would have to treat people the same, but the discrepancy in how you treat them shouldn't evident.

For instance, most people would walk away from a store that sent out its regular customers for the sake of a more prosperous customer. Such a store would lose people because they couldn't leverage the diversity between their standard and wealthy clients. Imagine you are in a group and you give attention more to a group member at the expense of others. You are not likely to get a satisfactory reply from others when you need feedback.

Chapter Three

How To Change 'No' Into A 'Hell, Yes'

Getting people to say yes to you is not as difficult as it seems. In the previous chapter, you have learned why they decline your proposal, reject your terms, and leave you in a relationship. The line between getting a yes and a no is very slim, but you can improve your chances of acceptance by leveraging the tips in this chapter.

Eliminating Limitations

There was a time I had the opportunity of meeting the CEO of one of the best marketing companies. I presented my ideas to him, but he wasn't impressed because of how I had explained to him. I used big words that bored him out, and I talked about the success of the idea vaguely. However, a colleague of mine pitched the same idea to him, and he got an appointment with the CEO. The difference between the two of us was that he explained in simple terms while I used complicated words. He talked with certainty about the success of the idea, and he was confident it would succeed. The line between getting a yes and a no is fragile.

The first thing to do if you want to get a yes from someone is to make what you are saying, appealing to the self-concept of the person. This is to say that the person you are talking to must feel involved in what you say. Self-concept simply has to do with the identity of someone, things that can be associated with someone, and the sense of being separated from others. Everyone wants to be treated with importance; what you have to say must appeal to the things that are important to the person you are saying it to.

Remember the earlier example of Hopkins and Schlitz. Schlitz purifies his beers just like all other brewers, but none of them talked about how their purity. Hopkins used this to make his advert that took Schlitz to the top of the chart. He made people feel like his product was the purest and the healthiest to drink among all others. In this example, Hopkins knew that people care for their health, which is vital to them. Perhaps those that didn't drink beer started drinking because the advert made it seem it was healthy for them.

Lessons From Insurance Companies

Insurance companies have so many customers because their insurance policies appeal to their self-concept. Many people want their properties safe. So, they don't mind paying what seems like stipends to guarantee that. Insurance companies give policies that make sure that their customers feel secured about their properties.

A car policy, for instance, is one of the ways insurance companies convince their customers to ensure their cars with them. They give policies like, "if your car gets stolen or damaged, giving you have paid certain beneficiary sums, we will get you a new car or fix the damage without any expenditure accruing to you." You can see that that is a tempting offer, and many people will want to jump at it because it appeals to their interest, which has to do with securing their properties.

There was a time at my place of work when some insurance agents came to advertise their policies. It was a health insurance policy. For a little over peanuts in our annual income, they offered to pay for the health services any worker would need if they ever fell sick. I'm still using the policy even though I don't work for the company again and many of us when they came. Their offer was able to influence us to accept their system because it appealed to our interest.

This means that if you want to persuade someone to listen to you and accept your views, you must think of what you can do to appeal to their self-interest. Create messages or instances that are dedicated to them. Instead of talking about how good your idea is, talk about how it would benefit them. For example, if you want to get a job or you want to get a promotion, you must be able to show them what they stand to gain if you were given that post. Also, if you wish to more customers as a businessman, create marketing messages dedicated to prospective clients. The messages shouldn't talk about the company, but about how the products can benefit them.

A Cue From Movie And Game Makers

Big companies with lots of customers seldom talk about how good and powerful they are. Besides, they rarely talk about the educational qualifications and capability of their workers. Instead, they talk about their products, features, and how they can add value to the lives of their customers.

Furthermore, most game enthusiasts watched the YouTube video session of the new PS5 that would be released very soon. There were great reviews and comments after the video session, and many people would buy the console. Why? It is simple. Sony didn't only show the customers that they can make video game consoles or that they have hired the best software engineers for their products.

Instead, they made their customers know that the new product would make them have a more natural like experience of their game. The company also informed buyers that they could play certain X-box games with the console and many more. Sony didn't only demonstrate that they have created another product; it also showed the customers the advantages of buying their latest game console.

More so, before Avengers End Game was released last year, many already bought tickets of cinemas that would be showing it. Why? It is just like what I have explained earlier. They created awareness that appealed to the target audience's interest in watching a fantasy movie of superheroes.

So, to be able to get desired responses, you must have something that would appeal to the interest of your audience. It would get you that promotion, the respect and appreciation you want from your kids, and the sales you wish to you to make. It will practically help you to achieve your goals. If you can't make your proposal appeal to the interest of the person you are giving it to, you can never get to persuade that person.

Always Offer Value

If you want to win over a person and sweep them off their feet, you must make them feel that whatever you are offering them is worth it. Top brands understand that offering value is the most practical and sustainable marketing strategy. When you purchase a top-quality product, you will tell your loved ones to buy it. Referrals will go a long way in establishing the authenticity of a product and build a company's image. Social media makes it easy to spread the news.

Nike, for example, endorses celebrities to increase the appeal of its products. Nonetheless, its high customer satisfaction is not built on this approach. The company offers some of the best quality shoes in the world. Nike uses good texture to develop its footwear. Besides, the interior is very soft, which gives comfort to the feet and makes you easily maneuver while wearing it. So, the success of this organization is primarily built on quality products and, secondarily, adverts.

Apple uses the same model. When it released its latest product, iPhone 11, it made the features appealing to the customers. Nonetheless, the vast sales were not just about its impressive marketing strategies but the exciting features of the phone. For example, the nature of the security of this new product makes it appealing to top people in the business world. Such individuals can be sure that their data is safe on this phone.

Over seventy-five percent of Americans lament that they have made an impulsive purchase. In other words, they bought products they never wanted or never planned to buy. This phenomenon is known as Post Purchase Cognitive Dissonance. They will feel that the purchase wasn't worth it later. This has put in their minds that they would not invest in similar products based on their past experiences. So, for you to convince them to buy your product, you must get your promotion right. Nevertheless, beyond the advert, you must be able to offer them products that provide them value.

Appeal To Logic

Appealing to emotions can help you gain attention, but it is not sustainable, especially if you are building long-term. You will lose relevance in no time if you do not present reasonable ideas. For instance, as a sales rep, your objective is to make sales. Nonetheless, you cannot achieve this goal without convincing prospective customers that the product is worth their investment.

You will have to highlight practical ways they will benefit by purchasing the item. Besides, you will also let them know why your product is superior to conventional ones. You may have to mention the ingredients in the product make it safe for them. Besides, you may have to explain that yours is cheaper than other options available in the market. You need to convince your clients that they will have no regrets if they invest in your product.

Leverage Selective Perception

Another thing you should take into consideration when speaking is selective perception. For instance, if a person who keeps fit but still smokes sees an advert on healthy books. It would not appeal to him at first, but if he sees a post that says the harms of smoking, he will click on the healthy book. It wasn't the book's advert that persuaded him to click on it; it was when his subconscious saw the harms of smoking that made him click.

What this example is trying to explain is that the man that smokes was drawn to the book because under the advert was the harm of what he does. Focusing on only what appeals to you is selective perception. To leverage selective perception, you need selective persuasion. In other words, you will submerge the main idea as the minute part of a bigger picture.

Big companies sometimes use particular persuasion in their adverts. I watched a Nike advert on YouTube a while ago. The setting was in Brazil. A boy was wearing a Nike soccer boot, and the rest weren't wearing anything; they were playing barefooted. In the advert, it was obvious the boy in the Nike soccer boot was a better player. He dribbled, passed, and shot better than the remaining boys. The company leveraged selective perception in this advert. Nike didn't say that playing soccer barefooted was a bad thing, but they did show that wearing Nike sneakers to play soccer would make you a better player.

Abraham Maslow's Hierarchy Of Needs

In some situations, the people you seek to convince might think that they do not need what you are offering them. According to Maslow, humans have a pyramid of needs, and the completion of one need would get us to the next. In the hierarchy, he said that at the bottom, we have the Physiological needs, which had to do with our basic needs as humans, e.g., Foot, clothing, and shelter. After that, we have safety, followed by Love/belonging, Esteem, and finally, Self-actualization - a level of need that not many people have achieved.

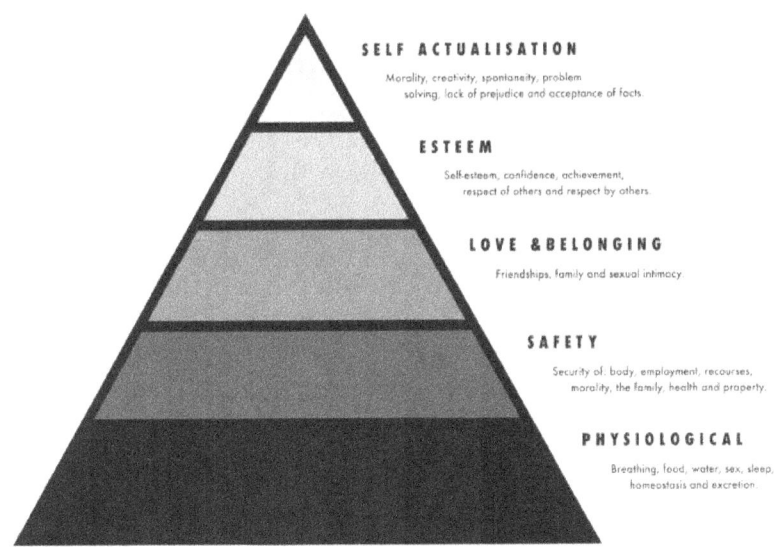

Figure 1: Abraham Maslow's Hierarchy of Needs. Credits: www.medium.com

According to Maslow, many people are in between the Safety/ Love or belonging pyramid. This is why you wouldn't persuade most people because they don't think they need what you are giving them. For example, if you are trying to get someone to purchase something that is meant for someone in the Esteem need, but what the person needed at the moment is in the Safety need, they would unequivocally say no to you.

However, you can still persuade them if you could conjure a logical argument, which would make them feel like they need what you are offering. For instance, in cases of couples or parents who haven't got life insurance and they don't feel like they needed it at the moment. You could, as a right insurance company agent posit this logical question to them: "What will happen to your partner or who would take care of your children if something was to happen to you?" They would immediately realize that they needed the insurance policy because it is sure that everyone would die, and nobody knows when they would meet with death.

Becoming A Gem Among Stones

It should also be noted that the person you are trying to persuade can access a plethora of things on what you are trying to convince him/her into doing. In 2000, shoppers at an upscale food market saw a display of twenty-four varieties of gourmet jam, and those that sampled it received a one-dollar coupon off the jam. Not very far away, there was another table that similar to the first one, but on this table were only six samples. What would happen? People would be less likely to buy from the second table, given that they have seen the first table.

You can stand out among your peers who do the same things through the following guidelines:

Be Heavily Reliant On Facts

If you want to earn the trust of people with your write-ups, you should be fact-reliant. For instance, if you're going to publish a motivational book or other write-ups, you must corroborate your arguments with facts. Moreover, if you want to impress your readers, you should base all the facts on the most up to date information. For example, if you're going to give a presentation on Google, you should use what they have done recently to win the applause of your audience.

To create a good impression, you should do enough research on what you are about to tell them. The words of experts on the issue would go a long way in helping you convince your readers. For instance, when writing about the advantages of consuming CBD products, you should cite studies that have proven that this substance is safe and has therapeutic effects.

It is also applicable in the academic field. If you are writing about the E=MC2 equation, you should include Albert Einstein and whatever he has said on the atomic bomb equation to corroborate your point. So, if you are trying to sell an idea, regardless of your field, you should always do adequate research on the topic and quote experts to solidify your claims.

Think About Potential Objections

One of the very best ways to impress your audience is to think about their objections. Have a foresight into what they might have against your work and remove them. For instance, if you are presenting a new idea to your company, think about possible areas of contention. Don't look at it from your perspective; look at it with the eyes of a critic.

It is just like how lawyers prepare their brief in a formidable manner. They would think of the likely objections the other counsel would raise, and they would block it out. SUITS, a law series, demonstrated this meticulousness in detail. In the series, two savant lawyers rub minds before they go for any matter - Harvey Spectre and Mike Ross.

They both stand as opposing counsels and fault all they have to say on the case in preparation for the court session. If you want to sway others, you must be your own staunchest critic. Scrutinize your work in the worst way possible, then block out anything that could serve as an objection. This approach will ensure that you will provide logical responses to both constructive and destructive critics.

Go All Out To Captivate Your Listeners Or Readers

Presenting facts is integral to the credibility of any presentation. Nonetheless, it can become dull and monotonous if you don't show it compellingly. Bring up an incident or a powerful statistic that would capture the mind of your readers. In most bestsellers, when you read the prologue, the story they would give you would encourage you to continue reading.

This is what most news outlets use in their headlines. They coin the words in such a way that you, as a reader, would want to know the body of the news. For example, if you're going to write a letter for promotion, you should start it with something colossal you have done for the company. It would serve as an incentive that would make your boss consider your request.

Furthermore, from the beginning of this book, you can see that I have been giving examples to make the explanations more comprehensive. If you want to persuade your readers as well, use a lot of illustrations and models that they can relate to in your book. For instance, if you are talking about politics, use current political leaders to corroborate your position.

Organize Your Points Systematically

You should organize your ideas and arguments logically and systematically. Note that the organization can be challenging when writing. Nonetheless, there is a simple way to do it. Start your discussion with the weakest, build on it, and end it with the strongest. Or, you may start your work with a generally accepted idea. Build well on it before moving to the ones your readers might oppose.

One crucial way to get a yes from your audience is if you finish your work with a very powerful and emotional appeal. Studies have shown that human beings are emotional creatures. So, while building on facts, an emotional appeal is also critical. There was this time that I watched a documentary on how one of the most notorious criminals was sent to the gas chamber.

When the prosecuting counsel was addressing the jury, he was so emotional that some of them were crying; I can remember he said; "...use the lives of the innocent that he has wasted to judge him, use the sorrow of the family he has bereaved to sentence him; a man like this cannot be left wandering on our street; who knows the next havoc he would wreck? The next life he would cut short? The next family he would bereave? The decision is in your hands..." Here, the lawyer stirred up emotion in the jury, and the man was finally sentenced to death. Be like that lawyer; emit emotions from your work; it would go a long way in affecting your audience.

Obstacles To Successful Persuasion

According to Kurt Mortensen, in his book Persuasion IQ, some obstacles hinder successful persuasion. They include:

- **Trying too hard:** - If someone doesn't really dig into what you are saying, move on. If you continue to linger and try harder than you should, the person would be turned off. Probably the person had been thinking about accepting your proposal. If they see you as too keen, they will begin to doubt you, and with time, they would leave you. So, if you don't want to be declined, you should know when to stop.

- **Not putting in the required effort:** - This is just like the first point, if you fail to input the necessary effort to convince the person, they would think you are not serious about what you are saying, or lazy. They would never buy into what you are telling them. You should put the effort in that is required to get what you want.

- **Making assumptions about your audience:** - You shouldn't assume what your audience is going to be. In the words of Albert Einstein, "Assumption is the lowest form of knowledge." Get to know your audience and interact with them on what you have known. Indeed, there are times you would have to assume about your audience, but you should keep in mind that new evidence about them could surface, and you should be ready to reassess.

- **Overrating yourself**: - You are supposed to be confident but do not be overconfident in your bid to persuade your audience. They will see you as pretentious, and this could be counterproductive. If you are overconfident, you will fail to hone your skills, and you will keep getting rejections. You are supposed to sit down and think hard about where your flaws are, and you should think about ways in which you can improve.

- **Forgetting about the importance of the whole conversation**: - You are supposed to engage your audience from the beginning of your conversation to sway them at heart. Do not stray, everything you say must be in line with the goal.

- **Not being prepared:** - There was this time I had a personal experience at failure because I wasn't prepared enough for a presentation. It was a college presentation, and I didn't study enough because I thought to myself, "How hard can it be?" When I got to the podium, I fumbled. If you don't want to perform woefully as I did in the face of your audience, you should be well prepared. If you aren't, they will see through you and think you value your time more than theirs.

- **Providing too much information:** - This is another way you hinder yourself from getting the right response. Just like the second point, you should tell them what they want to know. It would look like rocket science if you explain everything to them, but if you tell them what they need to know, then you would be able to make their decision-making easier.

Chapter Four

Importance Of Body Language

In a one-on-one conversation or public speaking, your gestures go a long way in determining your success. Your gestures can say more than your words. Therefore, it is vital to understand body language and how you can leverage it in your interpersonal and professional relationships. This chapter explores some of the crucial aspects of body language. However, for a detailed explanation of this concept, read "The Subtle Art Of Speed Reading People."

What Is Body Language?

While you are trying to convince your listeners, you might have done all that is necessary, but the audience will still not buy into your ideas. Why? Your body language might be putting them off. Your body language includes the way you position your feet, arm, face, and other body parts during a discussion. It can be your facial expressions or your leg positions. Body language is one of the things that turn people off from what you have to say. You must show them with your body language that you are confident about what you are saying. People do not like weakness, and once they sense it in you, they won't be convinced by anything you want to say.

The first impression matters a lot, and it is not your voice or how to talk that would strike people. It is how you carry yourself that would determine what kind of impression your audience will have of you. You should know that the kind of aura that hangs around you when you enter a room would determine how you would be attended to. For instance, if you exude confidence, people would most likely want to listen to you. However, if you display timidity, you might find it difficult to get the attention you crave.

Have you ever seen Mark Zuckerberg flinch when facing the camera? Have you ever seen Barack Obama stutter when addressing the public? The answers to the two questions would be no. For many successful people in business, political figures, and many more, one quality they all possess is confidence. What better way can they show it than through their body language?

How To Use Your Body Language To Persuade People

Communicating correctly with my body has helped me tremendously many times. For example, I was called for a job interview, and after we had done the exam, many of us passed. I got into the room where I met three stone-faced interviewers. I greeted them, and they instructed me to sit down. At first, I was very nervous, and my palm was sweaty.

Luckily, I remember something I read somewhere about confidence and what it would do for you. So, I inhaled heavily and exhaled in the same manner. When I was asked the first question, I answered flawlessly, and it caught their fancy. At the end of my session with them, one of the interviewers said he loved my confidence. A few weeks after the interview, I was given an appointment.

In the words of Barbara Pachter, "I believe that if you project an assured, credible and composed image, people will respond to you..." If you want to gain good attention, you must demonstrate confidence, credibility, and composure. If you can nurture yourself into these things, you will find it easy to make the right impression. There are various ways in which you can achieve a confident, composed, and credible body language. All other things fall in place when you have the confidence to attempt it. The following are some of what would help you to ooze out confidence via your body language:

Be Assertive

The first thing you should do to make your body language scream confidence is being assertive. According to Barbara Pachter, stand confidently; keep your legs aligned with your shoulders, and your feet approximately four to six inches apart. Distribute your weight equally on both legs, keep your shoulders back - but not way back - and turn your body towards others. This is what an assertive posture looks like - you stand tall and exude confidence.

A submissive posture can demonstrate humility when speaking to your superiors. However, it will give you out as some with low self-esteem when talking to your colleagues. Such gestures will not earn you respect in some settings. The presidential debate between Barack Obama and Mitt Romney demonstrated the benefits of assertiveness. When they started, they both had a good start, but towards the end, Obama floored him because he maintained an assertive posture, but Romney didn't. When the debate was going awry for Romney, he took a defeated stance, and people read into it. Obama read into it and continued to hammer on. It was part of why some people at the last minute were convinced to vote for him.

Avoid Using Submissive Sitting Positions

Make sure you avoid sitting in submissive positions. If you do, you show your audience that you don't have the confidence to address them, and they would not hear you. Even when they listen to you, they will not trust your counsels and submissions. This posture involves sitting down with your legs crossed, your arms folded in front of you, or with weight passed down on one hip. I watched a show where Keanu Reeves was interviewed. He sat down with confidence. It was written all over him, and many people, including me, wanted to hear the words coming out of his mouth.

Jack Ma, a famous Chinese businessman, is also an excellent example of sitting with assurance. The first time I watched his interview, I was so engrossed with what he said that I left my microwave on throughout the program. One of the things that drew me to him was the fact that he sat on his chair with authority. It is also applicable to the music and dance industry. We all get wowed by these rappers and singers with the way they walk, sit, squat, etc. They do all these things with confidence, and you should learn from them.

Consider Using Power Poses

During Amy Cuddy's TED talk in 2012, she said that two minutes of power poses could help you feel more confident.

She explained further that these poses help send a signal to your brain, which produces testosterone. They also lower your cortisol levels, which imply that they reduce your stress levels.

In trying to achieve an assertive posture, you need to stand tall and keep your posture open. If you stand tall, you portray a confident aura. However, you shouldn't puff your shoulders or heave your chest out. Standing tall makes your airway aligned to speak clearer and louder. Also, keeping your posture opened makes you seem more confident and trustworthy to your audience, which might have an effect on their subconscious, and they would want to listen to you.

Maintain Eye Contact

Being able to maintain appropriate eye contact reflects self-confidence. You don't see Mark Zuckerberg looking down at his toes when addressing an audience; neither do you see Hillary Clinton avoiding eye contact with those she is speaking with. Eye contact is a very crucial body language. If you can maintain eye contact, it means you are approachable, honest, and confident. You need to do this with whomever you are addressing, whether a person, two people, or a large crowd.

It is a body language that makes your audience trust you. People who can't maintain eye contact are either hiding something, uncomfortable, showing a lower status, or are being submissive. And if the audience finds any of these features, you will have a hard time convincing them. In the words of Michael Ellsberg, for eye contact to feel good, one person must not impose his visual will on another person. It should be a shared experience. You share feelings through eye contact with your audience. They see in your eyes, whether what you are saying is genuine or not.

It is more difficult to keep eye contact in large gatherings. If you find yourself in this position, focus on the key members of the audience. Do not take time, alternate through the room; this helps you to have a personal touch with your audience, which makes them vulnerable to persuasion.

Keep An Eye On Your Hands

You should also watch your hands when you are addressing your audience. According to Barbara Pachter, an essential part of mastering body language is to know what your hands are saying. When you are handling your audience, get your hands involved because it strengthens your points, and your audience would follow you. Take, for instance, if you are pitching a great idea to your bosses, your body language will count as part of the things that would persuade them to accept your opinion.

Use your hand to walk them through your ideas with your hand gestures carefully. However, it must not be too often because it would make you seem nervous or frantic. Note that some hand gestures could turn your audience off. For instance, putting your hand on your hips gives an aura of arrogance or impatience. Also, crossing your hand might pass the information that you are closed off, uncomfortable or defensive. These gestures can make your listeners uninterested in your ideas.

Leverage Facial Expressions

Another body language you should take note of is your facial expressions. When you want to address others, they want to feel accepted. They need to feel that there are some emotions behind your eyes. Most people have certain stern standard facial expressions, which make them less approachable.

There was a time some of my friends told me to smile often. They told me that they found it difficult to talk to me because of my facial expressions. You cannot convince others that you are approachable when you frown. Indeed, mean people smile sometimes. However, no one knows you without hearing, you speak. Meanwhile, you can appear endearing with your face language.

You must keep a loose facial expression if you want to have a positive impact on your audience. If you are talking to people, they tend to look at your face. If your face isn't appealing enough, you might not have the effect you want to have, which would persuade them, regardless of how detailed your presentation is. If you keep an endearing facial expression, you will sound more sincere, humane, and trustworthy.

According to Pachter, "there can be severe career consequences if you keep a severe standard facial expression. People may avoid you, think you are mad at them, or get defensive around you, and they are not good outcomes if you want to connect with them." If you want to connect with your audience, do not keep a possum facial expression; loosen your face. Smile often; it makes your listeners think you have nothing to worry about. If you smile at someone, they become comfortable and would probably smile back. Your audience wants to see that they can be comfortable around you. Meanwhile, getting them to feel comfortable around, you will go a long way in helping you persuade them because they will be ready to listen to you.

Move Freely

There are times when you will find yourself in a position to address a large crowd, e.g., TED talks, presentation of your idea to the board of directors, among many more. If you find yourself in such a situation, you should make sure you move freely. What do I mean? Note that when addressing an audience, a large one at that, you address them through the stage. You should know that the stage is your territory, use it. Do not make the mistake of staying in a place because it makes you look incompetent and scared. Move around the stage to look more natural, confident, and at ease with your surroundings, which would make you take your audience along.

If you watch shows where the speaker will have to stand up and address the audience, the more interesting ones move freely on the stage. You follow them with your eyes where they go, which keeps you more interested in whatever they say. The same is applicable if you are faced with a broad audience. Breathe in and out, and move freely in your surroundings. It shows that you are confident, and it allows you to project your voice in different manners.

Don't Fidget

When speaking to an audience, some postures make them think that you are fidgeting. Meanwhile, and if they feel you are not assured, they will doubt you. If you are someone that has fidgeting habits, like tapping your foot repeatedly on the ground, twirling your hair, or jingling something in your pocket, just to mention a few, you should work on yourself. These signs are sometimes seen as acts of nervousness, and like it has been discussed earlier, you don't want to be seen as nervous.

You should pay attention to these habits and improve yourself consciously because they may distract people from getting to know you, and that would take away from the message you are trying to pass across. Note these habits and work on changing them.

Mirroring Body Language

It is not your body language alone that matters; the body language of your audience also counts. If two people are talking, they both communicate in the language they both understand. Also, body language is used by people, not by just one person. What I am saying, in essence, is that if you want to bond with your audience, you should consider mirroring their body language to build acceptance and understanding.

Mirroring someone's body language is just reacting in the same manner as the person. For instance, if the person you are addressing sits in a particular position, you can mirror their body language by sitting in a similar position, or you can put on the expression on their faces or just their simple mannerism. It makes them feel comfortable around you and makes them talk freely to you and accept what you have to say. By mirroring their body language, they would think that you are similar to them.

However, timing is crucial when leveraging mirror body language. You should always know when to mirror the gestures of others. If you reflect someone's body language at the wrong time, they might think you are ridiculing them or poking fun at them. To succeed in mirroring other people's body language, you must make it feel and seem natural, not just to mimic or displease those you are talking to.

Use Firm Handshakes

One more thing we should know when we want to use our body language to persuade people is that we should have firm handshakes. Your input in the subconscious of the person you are trying to convince is your confidence, and they don't have anything to worry about. I have worked with a lot of successful people in business, CEOs, managers, etc. One thing is prevalent among all of them: they all give firm handshakes.

Once they grip your hands, you have this feeling that you can trust them even before you hear anything they have to say. If you want to persuade your listener, probably for a business meeting, a dinner, or any other gathering where you can meet people, your handshake must be firm enough to ooze confidence. However, don't make it too tight; it should be firm enough.

A large part of communication comes from body language, which includes facial expressions, handshakes, postures, among others. You should be conscious of the messages you pass via your body language. However, recognizing these body languages is not enough to persuade. You will have to do a lot of practice so that they would seem and appear natural enough.

A Short message from the Author:

Hey, are you enjoying the book? I'd love to hear your thoughts!

Many readers do not know how hard reviews are to come by, and how much they help an author.

If you can't remember how to do it, don't worry, I'll guide you: just open "Returns & Orders", scroll down to find the book. On the right side you will find as last button "Write a review for the product".

I would be incredibly grateful if you could take just 60 seconds to write a brief review on Amazon, even if it's just a few sentences!

Thank you for taking the time to share your thoughts!

Your review will genuinely make a difference for me and help gain exposure for my work.

CHAPTER FIVE

Listening Is Key

Many people like the sound of their voices; they'd prefer to say all they want to without giving a hoot about what the other person has to say. However, this approach will not endear you to others. This is one of the major turn-offs for people. According to Bernard M. Baruch, "Most successful people I've known are the ones who do more listening than talking." Listening is not an act; it is an art you have to master. This chapter looks at the benefits and importance of listening. You will also learn about some features that makes you a terrible listener.

The Art Of Listening

Many people do not realize that listening is a skill. Meanwhile, hearing is natural, but listening isn't. In other words, hearing does not require effort, but the same cannot be said about listening. One of the worst experiences I have ever heard came from a client of mine, who, before being followed by me, experienced this situation embarrassing enough to be taken as an example.

He was working with a marketing company. After a while he was talking and showing the slides of his PowerPoint presentation, he surprised the potential customer by snoring louder and louder. He was so busy making her buy the product that he didn't even stop for a moment to listen to what she wanted to tell him. If he had involved her and wasn't too interested in what he was saying, maybe he would have found it fascinating. In L. Ron Hubbard's words, the only way to entertain some people is to listen to them.

Listening is an important quality you need to succeed in your various relationships. If you want to enjoy more success when gaining the attention and approval of others, you need to develop your listening skills. Many of these big companies are not using magic or voodoo to persuade you to get their product; they listen to you to understand you and provide a product that would suit your taste. Listen to others, and you will see how you will convince them to do what you tell them.

I loved playing video games when I was younger, and I watched many videos on YouTube by game console developers about the next new game. There was this time I was going through the comment section of PS3 on YouTube, and I saw a post which was liked by many people about how unreal PS3 games were.

The customers said that Sony should make their game consoles strong enough to make their games more real. And in 2013, Sony released PS4 with a more realistic effect of the games. Many buyers, after the game console was released, gave very nice reviews. Sony got more customers to buy PS4 because they listened to that review of a fan and worked on it.

Listening To Keep Your Relationships Intact

You can only know what your loved ones want when you listen to them. Meanwhile, being able to satisfy the needs of others guarantees their loyalty and commitment to you. There was a time one of my many female friends came to me crying, asking me what to do about her boyfriend who was cheating on her with one of her friends. I am not an expert in handling romantic relationships, but I provided the tips she needed because I listened to her.

I just sat down for three hours and listened to how she suspected them and later how she found out that they saw each other. After she had told me everything, I just said that she should stay away from him and find happiness in other things because it was evident that he didn't respect her. She jumped on my advice immediately, and it later paid off for her.

As I said, I wasn't good with relationships, and it wasn't that my advice was top-notch. It was a line I picked from a movie I had watched. But what made her use my advice? Simple, I listened to all her rants. This is similar to all spheres in which you want to persuade your boss, your kids, your parents, your friends, among others. If you could take the time out to listen, you would be able to let them see reasons with you

In *"The Seven Habits of Highly Effective People"*, written by Steven Covey, I can remember the example of the CEO who had a problem getting his daughter to do anything he wanted. The man had a very terrible listening skill, and it affected his relationship with his daughter. However, after he reflected on what his wife told him that "He didn't listen her desires," and he sharpened his listening skills, he realized that his daughter started doing things the way he wanted.

Why Is Listening Important?

Listening has numerous benefits that can improve the quality of your life. Below are some the reasons it is essential to let others express themselves:

To Understand The Needs Of Others

For instance, you might want your friend to purchase a chocolate cake. If you haven't been listening to him/her, you cannot know that they have chocolate allergies. The person will most definitely decline to buy the cake. But, if you have been paying attention, you would know that there is an issue, to adopt a different approach, like "Wendy, I know you have chocolate allergies, but you can buy this cake for your nephew because he loves chocolate." Wendy will know that you care for her well-being and would think about your proposal, which is most likely that she would accept.

There was a time Charles, one of my clients, presented one of his brilliant ideas to a company where he was an employee. The board even commended the idea, but you know something? It was never accepted. Why? Simple, he wasn't listening to his boss. He told him that Charles should develop an idea for gaining more customers for a cereal producing company; instead, he gave an extensive presentation on how a cement company could gain more clients. His presentation was absurd, regardless of how detailed it was. His company didn't need it at the moment. So, his well-presented strategy was thrown out of the window.

Apple just doesn't develop a new gadget; they build their devices because of what their customers have said on the previous ones. In the same way, Nike doesn't just make new shoes because they can; they make new and better shoes because of the reviews they have got on the previous ones they made.

Listening Enables You To Learn More

You cannot learn by speaking because you will only hear to yourself. However, listening enables you to have more information about a topic or someone. It gives you the insight you never had and a new perspective on solving a problem. One statement of Larry King that I have always held on to is when he said, "I remind myself every morning: Nothing I say this day will teach me anything. So if I am going to learn, I must do it by listening."

Listening more to others would give you a lot of information about others. The data will be useful in the short or long run when you need to make decisions. Remember that the quality of your decision-making hinges on the information you have. Meanwhile, quality decision-making will help you to make good choices that will improve the quality of your life. In the words of Yogi Berra, "You can hear a lot just by listening."

Our world, as it is now, is information-driven. So, how much you know about those you want to persuade will go a long way in helping you sway them. How can you know about them if you don't listen to them? For instance, in a court of law, if a criminal matter is ongoing, the lawyers would have to listen attentively to what the witnesses, the opposing lawyer, and the accused say to persuade the judge to rule in their favor.

The more you listen, the more you will be able to gather critical facts about those that you want to persuade. Pay attention to what your boss wants for that project or what your kids have to say. Also, be willing to receive what your parents feel about your idea or what your customers have to say on your products. This simple habit can have tremendous effects on your working and interpersonal relationships.

It Helps You To Earn The Respect And Admiration Of Others

Another benefit of listening to others is that they will like you more. Many people in this generation do not really listen. Many people don't show a high level of attention to other people anymore; however, if you could show others that their opinion counts, it gives you an edge over the norm.

Many parents cannot get their kids to appreciate them or respect them because they don't listen to them. I can remember when I was growing up when I visited one of my cousins for Christmas. He was a nice young man, but he always has heated arguments and misunderstandings with his dad. There was the time I asked him why he hated his dad so much and didn't respect him at all. I can remember the answer he gave me, which would always ring in my head when I finally have my kids. He said, "That stupid man never listens to me. He thinks everything he says is what is right."

Like it has been explained earlier, people tend to talk more about themselves. So, if they can get someone to listen to their rants, when it is time for the listener to speak, they would be swayed. It is simple. If you show interest in the life of people and you allow them to talk about themselves, they will admire you. When you provide them with a piece of advice, you will quickly sweep them off their feet.

For instance, a couple of years ago, I met a lady at a conference I went for. From the way she conversed, you will instantly deduce that she has an introverted demeanor. I tried very hard to make her go out with me, and after several rejections, she accepted my invitation. When we got to the restaurant, she was shy to talk, but when I asked her questions about her and showed real interest in her life, she came out. She was going through a lot. She was raped, got pregnant, gave birth to the child who later died, and battled with cancer.

I gently held her eyes, looked into her eyes, and told her to hold on, and I also advised her to go to one of a top-grade doctor I know. She already told me that many people had reported her to visit different doctors that she wasn't ready to visit anyone. Still, she visited the doctor I recommended because I paid attention to what was happening to her.

It Nourishes Relationships

Most celebrities are liked and are listened to because they show that they listen to what other people say. There is this Instagram influencer called Kingbach. Many people get persuaded to buy things he posts on Instagram because he had shown them in many ways that he listens to them. For example, there was a time when he said he would do anything people told him and post a video about it. From the comment section, he did what they had suggested, and he posted a video about them. Kingbach would easily sway those whose suggestions get picked if he posted something, perhaps an advert saying they should buy something because he simply gave his followers a listening ear.

People seldom get someone who would want to listen to them because everyone is going through one thing or the other. Nonetheless, if you could find time to make others feel you care about what they are saying, they will find it easy to speak to you and grant your requests. Many reputable companies benefit from listening to their customers, which makes them rate them more. This strategy makes it easy for them to convince their clients to get their latest products. For instance, many top companies have links where customers could give suggestions. Most times, they use these suggestions, which earn them the admiration of their teeming customers.

It Reveals Deeper Meanings

Another benefit you seem to gain when you listen attentively to people is to get subtle messages and signs. Some people don't say everything about themselves, but from their demeanor, if you pay enough attention, you will pick pieces of information that will be easily missed. If you employ your observation skills and tap into your intuitive senses, you will be able to get less obvious facts quickly.

For instance, if you are trying to get a customer to buy a product, if you pay enough attention, you will know from the subtle signs that they will give you whether or not they have been swayed. Some would be grumbling, muttering, or making faces that pass across information about their state of mind, and the only way you can get this is if you pay enough attention to them.

There was a time I interned at an organization where I was assigned to a company that sold baby products. I was given the guide job. A lovely lady entered the store to buy diapers for her baby but didn't know which one to buy. I walked up to her and asked what she wanted to buy, and she told me that she wanted a diaper for her child. I asked which product she had in mind. She said she didn't know. I took her to the diaper section, and I started showing her a series of diapers. As we passed each section, she made some faces, which meant she disapproved of them. There was a time we came upon the best, but her grumbling told she didn't want to get it. I didn't force any on her; she later bought the one she felt was the best for her child.

This example is merely trying to explain that if I hadn't been paying attention to her, I wouldn't have seen those expressions on her on the face. I would have dwelled on the one I thought was best, and she might end up not buying any.

What Makes You A Bad Listener?

The more you try to listen, the more you'll realize how difficult it is. Many things serve as an obstruction for listening attentively. It may be consciously or subconsciously. The more you do these things, the worse you get at paying attention and convincing others. Consciously stop the following habits that have negative impacts on your listening skills:

Lack Of Focus

One of the most common things that get us easily distracted from listening is not focusing. Focus is a critical aspect of listening. If you want to get information, endear yourself to a person, pick subtle signals from the speaker, you must be focused when listening. Many people lose focus almost immediately. They start a conversation with another person.

Perhaps what the person has to say is boring, or what they are saying is of little concern to you. In such situations, we get easily distracted and space out. It is a subconscious thing. Most people do not know when they slip away from their speaker and start doing something entirely different, taking their minds away from whatever the speaker says.

I can remember one of my first dates. I was 17, and I picked Lia at her house, and we went to one of the best Chinese restaurants in town. We entered, and we ate before small talks began. I wanted her to be my girlfriend, but we ended up as friends because of my lousy listening habit of losing focus if the issue is of little consequence to me.

She started talking about Balles and Ballerinas, which was boring for me. I spaced out, looking out of the window at moving cars, and it was the snap of her fingers that jeered me back. She liked me, but she said she couldn't date me because I don't seem like I would be able to focus on important things in life. Such experiences have made me improved my listening skills. I realized that being charming and intelligent are not good enough attributes to keep relationships.

Also, there was a client counseling interview I watched some years back. When the client told the lawyer what she was going through, the lawyer was doodling on a sheet of paper lying on the table. The client carried her bag and walked out of the lawyer's office, fuming that he wasn't good enough to handle her matter. Why did she leave? He wasn't focused enough on what exactly was the legal problem of the lady; instead, he lost focus; perhaps the part of the law that affected the lady was boring. He started doodling and lost the opportunity to handle the case because of his bad attitude to the client's concern. So, avoid this bad habit.

Don't Be Sentimental

Another huge barrier to good listening is when you are bias or prejudicial. Many people are biased by age, race, religion, past experiences, gender, just to mention a few. These sentiments will hinder you from ever listening to those you are prejudiced towards and would find it very difficult to relate with them.

For example, there was footage I watched. A woman who wanted a Mexican to buy her product couldn't get her to buy because she was a little bit prejudiced toward the race. The Mexican woman had entered the store to buy a particular body cream, and when she was trying to explain to the guide, it was evident that she wasn't ready to listen to her. She had a disgusted look on her face because her customer was Mexican. The customer stormed out of the store because she felt unaccepted and unwelcomed.

Many of us are also biased when it comes to the attractiveness of our speakers. Most people find it easy to listen to attractive people, and that is one of the reasons people turn up big for Arianda Grande's concert. It is just us being humans. However, we find it very difficult to listen to plain people. We pay attention to the physical appearance of our communicator and how we feel about them. However, it is not every time we get to see people that would appeal to our eyes, and we will need to persuade those that don't. What would you do if you see someone that doesn't appeal to you? Don't you make that sale? Don't you get that promotion?

Don't Have Preconceived Notions

Also, many have preconceived ideas and biases about a particular issue, which makes listening to another opinion on the same matter difficult. We are not open-minded enough to accommodate the views of others. When they say something different, we object, and we become obstinate, no matter the logical argument they bring.

If we want to appeal to others, we may not accept what they say, but we must listen enough and attempt to understand them. This approach will let them see that you have a different opinion, but you still tried to see theirs, which would make them want to reciprocate by listening to you. Before you know it, they would accept your proposals.

Greg, a friend I had during my internship with a firm, was a really stubborn guy. We were all told to present an effective strategy to improve sales in the tech sector. Our instructor gave us a way in which we should go about providing the pitch if we wanted it to be accepted. My friend felt the instructor's method was quaint, so he came up with his way. It was an excellent presentation by my standard, but it was rejected. Why? It is obvious, isn't it? He didn't listen to what the instructor told us. He had a preconceived idea on how to give his pitch, which was very excellent but was still rejected.

Avoid Hasty Judgment

In relation to being prejudiced towards people, which hinders our ability to listen attentively, we also judge. This means that many of us, after seeing our communicator, we already start thinking about how, for instance, how underqualified the person is, how dim-witted they are. This attitude affects the way we listen to them and, eventually, how we regard them.

For example, when most of us think that a person isn't on the same level of smartness, we tend to switch off. We just want to show them how smart we are and point out to them that there is no point in listening to them. However, if we don't listen to them, there is no way we will be able to know what they needed and how we could encourage them to go for our option.

Avoid Listening To Different People At The Same Time

Sometimes, we don't give our adequate attention to those we want to persuade because we listen to more than one conversation at a time. This is a habit that will ensure that you don't get the best out of interactions. Meanwhile, robust relationships are built on quality conversations. Once you often lose focus when listening to a person, you are already creating gaps in the relationship. This culture can ruin your marriage, relationship with your kids and make your employee treat you harshly.

There was a day Alexa - one of the most one of the best secretaries I have ever known - needed to do something for his boss at her first place of work. She was on a call, and at the same time, she was trying to listen to him. He wanted Alexa to deliver a package for him, and Philip - her husband - was on the phone, asking her to get some groceries on her way home back. After the discussions, Alexa couldn't remember what they both told her to do for them. If she had delivered the package for her boss, Alexa would have got a good recommendation from him, but since she ignored him when he was talking to her, Alexa, due to her lack of experience, lost it all.

This point is somewhat similar to the focus point I made earlier. You need to focus on one person at a time for you to get the best out of the discussion. Don't overrate yourself. If you try to juggle more than one at a time, you could end up not gaining anything from the conversation.

We should also consider that non-verbal signs can also show your communicator that you aren't listening to them. Many might even be listening attentively, but their gestures may depict otherwise. You should also make a conscious effort to leverage body language, which signifies that you are listening. Some of the signs that demonstrate that you are not listening include lack of appropriate posture, not maintaining constant eye contact, not giving the apt expressions, among other signs.

Don't Give Selfish Feedback

To convince someone that you are paying attention, you must know how to give the right feedback. For example, if someone had confided in you about the terrible state of their relationship. If you want to persuade them to buy a dress from you, the timely feedback in that instant would be something like: "Hey, why don't you try on this new dress? It might take your mind off him/her." You would be marveled at how they would jump at the proposal.

We weren't given birth with how to provide feedback in situations, but we could learn a few tips that would help us to develop how we give feedbacks in cases. Taking the pain to listen to someone would be futile if you can't come up with the right feedback. The first thing you should know giving feedback is that you should be as specific as possible. If you talk in vague terms, the person will find it hard to figure you out. If the situation is critical, the person tends to turn you down. When trying to give feedback, you should try and point out specific behavior or specific occasion out of what you've been able to pick when you were listening.

For example, in case you have a customer that wants to buy a product from your store. After listening, you could chip in with your reply with something like: "You said earlier that..." This would make them feel you have listened to them and would think you have their best interest at heart, which would make them want to do what you tell them.

Pick Your Moment

Also, when giving feedback, you should pick your moment. What do I mean by choosing your moment? It means you should be aware of the state of mind of your communicator before you should give feedback. For example, if an angry customer enters your store with a complaint about one of your products. Even though you have listened to his criticism, you should try and calm him down a bit before giving him feedback because an angry person tends to reject everything said to them. So, let the person calm down before you speak to them to avoid a transfer of aggression.

Chapter Six

Persuasion In The Political World

Do you ever wonder why people still vote even with the knowledge that most of what has been said in the manifestoes would not be fulfilled? Even with the rigors of voting, they always go to cast their votes. Despite the knowledge of the constant failure of the election cycle, they still go out en mass to vote. The answer to these questions is simple: because the candidate has persuaded them to vote.

People accepted significant political figures like Dalai Lama, Abraham Lincoln, Nelson Mandela, Winston Churchill, and others because they could convince people that they were the right candidates for the position. We will be looking into specific political figures and how they have persuaded people to accept them in this chapter.

Witty Winston Churchill

The first political figure we will access is Winston Churchill, the former Prime Minister of the United Kingdom (1940-1945, and 1951-1955). He is deemed to be one of the most outstanding leaders in the 20th century. Not only did he lead the UK throughout the second world war, but he was also known to be a good orator and won a Nobel Prize in Literature in 1953. He has various ways of giving speeches that have swayed people off their feet.

If you have an aspiration of being a political giant like Churchill, here are some tips you could use and make your political dream come true:

Crisp And Precise Statements

The first tip from what I have learned from Churchill is that your sentences and statements should be pleasant and short. If you want to motivate people to vote for you, endeavor to be short, enjoyable, and direct. If you search the internet for his speeches, you will find out that whenever he was talking, he was concise, crisp, and direct with his statements. He has the habit of addressing the issue immediately without beating around the bush.

Most of Churchill's presentation passed his messages immediately with efficacy to his audience, which was why he had many admirers. There was a time I went to a rally, and the Mayor was asked to come and give a speech. He started by greeting and praising everyone, which got the attention of everyone. However, perhaps those who wrote his script for him weren't professionals. Before he got to address the issue, most of the people present had either lost interest or struggling to focus. His speech wasn't concise, and it didn't address the issue on time.

If you want to earn plaudits through your speech, just like this political icon, you must learn how to be crispy and short with your sentences. Although most people think using short, crisp, concise, and direct sentences would put off their listeners, if it is done right, you will sweep them off their feet.

The quote Churchill gave during his speech when addressing Harrow school is a perfect example of his approach. His use of repetition made it easy for his audience to grasp what he was driving at.

"Never give in. Never give in. in anything, great or small, large or pretty, never give in, except to conviction of honor and good sense."

This speech is non-exhaustive and precise. He told his audience not to give in no matter the situation they were going through. This speech was so good that it caught the attention of the listeners by its sheer precision. Inevitably, the audience responded with a standing ovation.

Leverage Repetition Appropriately

Another key element you must incorporate into your speech is Repetition. Some people may find this redundant and entirely unnecessary, but most people tend to forget things easily. So, your emphasis on the issue makes it easy to keep your words in their memory. For example, his famous speech, *"We shall fight in beaches."*

"We shall fight on the beaches. We shall fight on the landing grounds. We shall fight in the fields, and in the streets, we shall fight in the hills. We shall never surrender."

This speech was forthright, short, and straight to the point. Besides, he used repetition to emphasize the fact that it would require their collective efforts to drive the Germans away and emerge victoriously. Most reputable and successful political figures have this same approach. Repetition puts your audience in the mood and allows them to see what you are driving at quickly.

An excellent example of a repetitive speech is Martin Luther King Jnr's "I have a dream." You might have read the speech or heard it read at a particular period in your life. From the speech, Martin Luther King Jnr kept repeating the phrase, ***"I have a dream."*** He was trying to create a future where there would be no more racism, and his speech swayed many people.

Many cried while many reflected. The repetition of the phrase set many of his audiences in the future that would be free from racism. After the speech, many saw the evil of racism and sought for it to reduce. If you want to become a political figure just like Churchill, you should be willing to do the things he did. One of them is the art of leveraging repetition to devastating effect.

Take Advantage Of Excellent Rhetoric

Another element that makes Winston Churchill one of the best orators of his time was that he uses a lot of rhetoric in his speeches. He asked his audience open-ended questions, which pulls them into what he was saying. Asking rhetorical questions gets your audience more involved with what you are saying. They won't only listen to you, but also reason along with your logic. Rhetoric is simply just the use of language to influence the actions and thoughts of your audience.

According to Connolly, a speaker must appeal to will and reason. However, also to the delight, by presenting thoughts in style as pleasing as it is clear, and in a tone appropriate to his subject and audience. This is a concise explanation of leveraging the magic of rhetoric. You make your audience more involved in what you are saying when you ask them rhetorical questions in your speech. For instance, Dan Brown's "*Deception Point*" vividly demonstrates how a speaker can win the heart of the listeners by leveraging rhetoric. In the book, there is a character who is a senator and wants to run for the presidential position.

He was able to sway people to his view when he asked them a series of rhetorical questions when giving speeches. He was trying to get the people to reject the president he was running against because the president gave ridiculous amounts of money to NASA who hadn't given any result in return. There was one he asked; ***"What would happen to our children's education if we continue to fund NASA that has nothing to show for our money?"*** He was able to sway the citizens because he could take them along in his speech, not only in words but in reasoning as well.

Be Concerned About The Affairs Of The Listeners

Another key lesson to learn from Churchill is his uncanny ability to address issues regarding the welfare of his audience. His words showed that he cares about them. Endeavor to say what is on the mind of the audience. Address the issue bothering them. You shouldn't speak to the audience; you should speak for them.

This has to do with your use of words. When speaking to your audience, especially when you have political aspirations, you should use less of ***"you"*** and more of ***"we."*** What do I mean? Winston Churchill, in his speeches, used a lot of *"we"* rather than *"you."* This is evident in his speeches, especially one of the most celebrated *"we shall fight in the beaches."*

"... we shall prove ourselves once again able to defend our island home..."

If you want to earn favorable responses with your speeches, you must be a master of language a non-specialist would understand. The citizens of Britain, during the time of Churchill, listened and got motivated and inspired quickly by him because he spoke for them instead of talking to them.

What people want is a representation, not only information. If you could show them that you represent them in your speeches, you will find it easier to persuade them to accept your view. For example, I watched a live speech given by the current Prime Minister of Britain, Boris Johnson. He spoke on the looting and nuisance taking place in the country about the worldwide protest on the unlawful killing of George Floyd.

He started his speech by saying that he felt what the people were feeling and the injustice that had taken place. He went on to praise his people and commend their outcry for justice, but he switched by saying that the looting and other criminal activities that are being orchestrated is done by some of the citizens who would make others suffer. He explained that only the people could stop this mayhem.

I remember vividly that throughout his speech, he uses the term "*we*" instead of "*you*" because he knows it would be easier to persuade his people by talking for them and including them rather than speaking to them and accusing them. After his live speech, I read that Britain witnessed a reduction in these crimes that have been carried out under the facade of protest.

If you know how to address your audience by talking for them, speaking out what they wanted deep down, they would respond much better to you. Also, you would find it easier to persuade them. So, you must prioritize representation.

Exude Confidence

If you want to persuade your audience, you must speak for them in a way that shows genuineness and assurance. People want to believe that what you are saying is authentic and that you are confident in your prowess of proffering a solution. Winston Churchill, in most of his speeches, appeared to be very secure and genuine, which made people believe in him. A superb example of his speech that made his sway his audience is *"Finest Hour."*

"Hitler knows that he will have to break us in these islands or lose the war. If we stand up to him, all Europe may be freed, and life or the world may move forward into broad, sunlit uplands."

In this speech, he put the minds of his people at ease by what he said. He showed Hitler to his audience as a fearful man that might lose the war if he wasn't able to invade Britain. Also, he made it sure to his audience that invading Britain would be a very tough task, herculean for even Hitler. This made people trust him so much that whenever he gives out a command stating that something should be done, people readily accepted.

What you should learn from this is that if you want to convince your audience, you should be able to ooze confidence that would make them believe in you to be able to carry out what you are saying. Do you think people just vote because the candidate is handsome or beautiful, or has a magnificent voice? No, these qualities might add to your acceptance. However, what you have to say must show that you know what you are saying, confident that you would carry it out.

What worked most for Churchill was that he was somewhat a military man, and he was appointed to lead the country through the war. So, people were sure that he would be able to lead the country to victory. Most of us are not even experts at what we are trying to persuade people. However, just like Churchill, engage your audience with authenticity and confidence. Another element that made him turn out to be an excellent political figure is his ability to bring out the right emotion in his audience. There was a time when he was giving a speech that he was close to tears as he gave the speech. It showed people who were listening to him how affectionate he could be.

Nelson Mandela

Another political figure that used his persuasive prowess to become great is Nelson Mandela (1918-2013). He was a man that suffered the apartheid in South Africa, was jailed, and later became the president of the country. When I was younger, I had always wondered how he did it. I could not understand how he got the whites in South Africa to accept the Black and colored as equals, even to how they allowed him to rule over them. It was when I became older that I realized that he made them see that he was the perfect choice for the position.

Nelson Mandela was arrested and imprisoned for twenty-seven years before he was released and took charge of the negotiation that led to the quenching of the civil war that was already brewing in South Africa. Why was a man in prison released and appointed to handle the negotiations before the civil war broke out? Why was he followed by the oppressed group when he was appointed to see to the negotiations? It was because he was able to persuade them that what he's got was the best option for both parties. The following lessons can be learned from this great man:

Show Genuine Care For Your Target Audience

From Mandela's story, I learned that you must really care for your audience. It should be obvious in the way you talk that they matter to you. He went to prison for twenty-seven years because he cared enough for his people. He wanted neither white supremacy nor black domination, but equal society, and he showed his care by even putting his life on the line for what he cared about.

Now, I am not saying that you should start endangering yourself because you want to persuade people, especially politically. Nonetheless, you are just to show that you care for the well-being of your listeners when speaking. Mandela was formally a peaceful protester against the apartheid system in South Africa, propagating equality between both races. However, he realized that if some drastic actions are not taken, the war against apartheid wouldn't be won. He started co-funding the militant Umkhonto we Sizwe.

He was arrested and sentenced to life imprisonment. On a normal circumstance, he was to be killed; but Nelson Mandela went to the extreme to show that he really cared about stopping apartheid and foster racial equality. This is one reason why the former president thought he was the best man for the negotiation to curb the civil war. There was a time when he used one of his trials to show in his speech that he cared about what he had been supporting. He had been charged with three counts of sabotage.

"During my lifetime, I have dedicated myself to this struggle of the African people. I have fought against white domination, and I have fought against black domination. I have cherished the ideal of a democratic and free society in which all persons live together in harmony and with equal opportunities. It is an ideal which I hope to live for and to achieve. But if needs be, it is an ideal for which I am prepared to die."

From this speech, Nelson Mandela was able to tell the whole world he cared enough for stopping the apartheid system that he is ready to die for it. You get to win over critics just like him if you could show people you care about what you are saying. They must believe that you have their best interest at heart. If you could show them that, you get to sway them to accepting your view readily.

Be Deliberate In Your Interactions

Another reason why Mandela was such an inspirational political figure is that he conversed deliberately. He made his grounds clear; he doesn't cut corners. He comes out clean with whatever he has to say. When President F.W. de

Klerk released Nelson Mandela, he had at the back of his mind plans to favor the white minority for the negotiation. However, Nelson Mandela had a different take; he wanted everyone to be equal. For this reason, the negotiation to end the civil war tension took four years before both parties came to a consensus.

He joined the ANC anti-colonial group, and he later co-founded Youth League to eradicate the apartheid supporting white only Nation Party. He involved himself in many things to stop the apartheid culture, including his involvement in the Defiance Campaign in 1952 and many more. He even went as much as secretly joining the already banned South African Communist Party to achieve his objective.

If you want to win over people, you should make sure you show them that you are devoted to the cause. Make them feel you are in it with them. Why is it that the black community in the country supports black politicians? Because they think that the brother is always passing through or have passed through the struggle, and they would believe that having him there would be better for them.

Mandela showed in various instances that he was a committed man to the liberation of the blacks in South Africa through his speeches and multiple associations. If you want to have more success getting people to agree with you, always show them through your speeches, actions, and association that you are committed to their cause. Be like Mandela, whose commitments made South Africa carry-out the first multi-racial election, which saw him emerge as the first black president of South Africa and a Nobel laureate of Peace.

Abraham Lincoln

A tremendous political figure that should not be left out on this persuasion parade is Abraham Lincoln. He was renowned for using three minutes and two hundred and seventy-three words to make people see the catastrophe war causes. He also inspired his listeners to dedicate a cemetery to the forty-six thousand soldiers who died in the civil war.

Just a month after Abraham Lincoln was pronounced the President of the country, the USA plunged into a civil war that claimed the lives of many. Gettysburg, one of the bloodiest places where the battle took place, was the location of one of his best speeches. For the fallen, Abraham Lincoln was called on to give a speech to honor the dead forty-six thousand soldiers that died because of the war. From his address that moved many, I was able to learn some things about persuasion. Here they are:

Find Common Ground

The first thing is that you should find an agreement ground where your audiences can agree and neglect their various beliefs. For example, if you are running for a political post, you have to persuade a crowd of whites, blacks, Latinas, and the other races. You can't start with a racial matter because most certainly, they all hold various views on racial issues. You should find a better field like tourism, economy, and other things that they all agree on.

Abraham Lincoln, when trying to get the people of America to stop the civil war, during his Gettysburg speech, he went back eighty-seven years to remind his people how and why they came to become an independent state. He further used phrases like "All men are created equal," something they all agreed on. He reminded them that it was because of liberty and equality that they drove the Britons out of their lands. So, why is it that they are still shedding each other's blood that they fought so hard to gain freedom? He could bring his people to a leverage ground of agreement, not showing favor to any side.

This made me remember one time in college when the students debated the aspiring student President. We were all pumped up to know what these guys had in stock for us. The interviewer asked the most popular candidate a question, which made him later lose the election. The interviewer asked him how he would handle the accommodation issue, how will he take it with the school management because not all our halls are in the right conditions. He answered that we would raise money. Many people immediately disagreed with him.

He could have come up with a better and vague answer like, "We will address the matter with the school management." However, he stood firmly on the side of the school management – or so it seemed. The point of this example is that if you find yourself in the position of persuading people with conflicting interests, make sure you start whatever you have to say on a bare ground in which the two parties hold no grudges.

Leverage Illustrations

Also, convincing people, you should make it a habit to start with a story or chip in a story. When Abraham Lincoln was giving his speech at Gettysburg, he started with the story of the struggle of those that liberated America, which the war was then destroying. He pricked their conscience just like asking them how they would have liked it if they had created something with sweat and hard labor, only for their offspring to start destroying it.

"Four score and seven years ago, our fathers brought forth this continent, a new nation, conceived in liberty, and dedicated to the proposition that all men are created equal."

He started his speech with an emotional story that moved his audience. It was the same thing that the Britons did to them that they were at the time doing to themselves. Therefore, if you want to make others accept your view on a particular issue, you should try and start with a story. Moreover, research has shown that speeches that begin with stories have higher tendencies of influencing the listeners.

During my college days, my roommate went for a debate competition, and he and his team lost. I knew my friend was an outstanding and aggressive debater who always has his facts right before he starts the debate. I met him and asked him why he lost. The reply he gave me was that he and his team weren't able to match the opponent in instilling emotions in the audience and judges. I was at first perplexed at his reply, but I further asked him what he meant. He explained that the two teams were evenly matched when it came to facts – they both had their points right. However, what gave the other team edge over them was that they started presenting their facts with stories. He told me that his team just started giving facts, but the other team came up with convincing stories that went in line with their points.

According to James Pennebaker in his book, *The Secret Life of Pronouns,* "In any interaction between two people, the person with the higher status uses fewer I-words..." This is applicable to all the political figures that have been mentioned; they all used words like "we, us, our..." So, if you want to persuade your audience, you must learn the art of using less of the first-person singular pronoun (I) and start using the first-person plural pronouns (us, our, we). Winston Churchill, Nelson Mandela, Abraham Lincoln, Dalai Lama, and other significant political figures adopt this means in speaking with their audience, and it has worked effectively for them.

Chapter Seven

Influence Is About Perception

According to the Merriam Webster dictionary, influence can be said to be the power to change or affect someone or something: the ability to cause changes without directly forcing them to happen. And it defined perception as the way you think about or understand someone or something.

If you seek to gain the approval of your audience, you must be conscious of these two concepts. This is because, as the definitions entail, you are to cause changes in the person you want to persuade via what you understand about that person. So, influence is about perception. From all I have explained from chapter one, you would have noticed that you know or think about someone that would determine whether or not you would convince them. This chapter will review how you can influence people by changing their perception.

Influence By Sight

Most of us are influenced by what we see on the internet, and top brands have cultivated the habit of using it to their advantage – getting you to buy their products. They all know that if you see one of your influencers using their products, it will stir you to think about purchasing their product. They influenced your decision, changing the way you see their products. They successfully convince you that you will have a good life like the model when consuming their products.

If we want to persuade people, we must be concerned about taking practical steps to affect their perception. You might have heard "internet influencers" before. They are those that can affect your thinking, in as much as you are still on the internet. They post themselves living in luxury, fancy vacations, wearing the latest clothing materials, and many other attractive things. They do all these to get you on their sides so that when they have a proposal, you will jump on it without thinking.

For instance, if someone had been posting about how luxuriously they have been living, which had always fascinated you. If the person just drops a link, saying that they got a handful of the money they are using to sponsor their luxurious life from it. Many people would likely jump at it. In such a situation, they have influenced your decision by what they perceive you to want.

However, not all these internet influencers are living the lives they claim to be living; most of them are living a fake life, posting lies to intrigue their fans. The story of Byron Denton, the nineteen-year-old, showed how easy it was to fake a living. He is a blogger based in London who wanted to test how easy it was to fake a life on Instagram, and he was surprised at how people can be easily swayed by phony living. The young man posted an edited picture of himself sitting in a private jet, which immediately got him over a thousand likes in seven seconds. He said when he saw that George Mason fake a vacation and many other people, he decided to give it a trial. They all manipulate information to get your attention.

Many influencers live fake lives just to gain attention, just like Byron's theory. They get you thinking, "I wish I were that guy." Consequently, whenever they bring something to you, you might jump at it without overthinking it. Some influencers show things that aren't even in existence, like when Taylor Evans said her Miami vacation was sponsored.

How To Change The Perception Of Others

If you want to sway people with ease, you should have at the back of your mind that the person's perception matters. In order to have more success in changing your listener's view, the following tips will be helpful:

Note Preferences And Background

The first thing that you should know if you want to be more sensitive to your listener's view is that you should be aware of your preferences and background. According to Miner, people come to any situation with a different set of lenses based on their experiences and culture. Your experience in life is different from that of others, and you must never forget that. Meanwhile, their exposure affects their cravings and judgment of situations.

If you want to change their view, you should find a way to get to know their background and preferences. For instance, someone that earns less than five thousand dollars would find buying a phone or laptop worth a thousand dollars a little bit too much for them. If you want them to buy the phone or laptop, and you just drop the price on them, they would not buy it. But, if you find time to get to know them, engage them, and they tell you about their preference or background, you would know how to go about the situation better. For example, you can point out the way the one thousand dollars phone can improve their lives, and you'd be surprised at how they would jump at your offer.

Pay Attention To Their Body Language

You must be aware of non-verbal signs. Miner said that top employees aren't exceptionally smarter, but they are just emotionally intelligent and hugely perceptive. They find non-verbal signals, which many people don't know that they are giving. These cues give away their state of mind. However, they are easily missed by most.

For instance, when offering a product to a prospective customer, you can know when the customer's body language is screaming no by being observant. You can tell from something like poor eye contact, crossed arms, among others that something is wrong. Noticing these signs will enable you to change your tactics on time.

Improve Your Listening Skills

The importance of excellent listening skills cannot be overemphasized. You must hone your listening skills for you to get all the necessary information out of your speaker. I have discussed why listening is critical in the previous chapters, so I would not explain further on it again. You should create a conversation that is open-minded so that you can learn. Listening makes you get to learn exciting things about the speaker. It is when you listen that you get to know the preferences and background of those that you are trying to persuade, and it is also via listening that you will be able to catch those non-verbal signs.

"You have to go in with big ears and smallmouth..." Miner.

Manipulation Or Influence?

Now, I don't want us to confuse influence with manipulation (manipulation of information), albeit, the latter would be explicitly discussed in the next chapter. The two concepts are similar, but not the same. Manipulation controls someone or something to the manipulator's advantage, and influence has to do with changing or affecting someone without directly forcing them to happen.

You should, however, know that most of the stories that spur us into action are a result of deliberately tweaking information. The one giving the report gives the information in a way that favors him, regardless of withholding any valuable information. This is what happens most times in courts; the lawyer manipulates information that favors his client. There was a lawsuit I watched on the television where the accused was charged with murder.

The prosecution lawyer knew well that the accused was not the one that killed the deceased, but he withheld that information because the accused was present at the time the murder occurred, and he had the motive to kill the dead. The accused was sentenced to death for the crime he didn't commit. In such an instance, the lawyer "edited" the information to favor his claims, and he was able to persuade the judge to convict the accused.

Manipulation of information is another mode of persuasion. However, this time, it is different because the manipulator is not coming clean with all the information. It is an excellent strategy to get people to do what you want because they would hear what you want them to understand. Do you ever remember when you were smaller, and you fought with your sibling? When you were narrating your story to your parent, did you mention that you attacked your sibling? No, and that is the simple term of tweaking information. You wanted your sibling to be punished, but not you.

Many news agencies apply this strategy. They write what they want the public to hear, not necessarily divulging all the information. I just realized some years ago that whenever a disaster, accident, or something terrible happened, which resulted in casualties, the news agency never reveals the real number of the losses. The essence of changing the narrative is to change the view and decision of a person. The manipulator thinks or knows that people would react in a certain way if all the information is divulged. So, they hold onto the part that they feel wouldn't allow the people to behave in a way that is contrary to what they want to achieve.

Protection Or Lies?

There are many movies in which the government decides not to tell the citizens of a particular problem until they have solved it or it got out of hands. They know that if they divulge valuable pieces of information that would throw the public into pandemonium, there would be a catastrophe. Meanwhile, this is against the peace and order the government is supposed to maintain.

Many people are involved in the changing narratives in this age, and the internet has fostered it. Someone would just sit down in their rooms and post on the internet, and people would take it up without actually finding the truth. Many social media users even manipulate information to the extent that they don't add authenticity again. For instance, the case of the lady that said Justin Beiber raped her is a clear example of how people can make blatant claims, regardless of its consequences.

However, in as much as manipulation is very efficient in getting people to do what you want of them, it might bounce back, affecting you adversely. For instance, the lawyer I watched earlier where the lawyer got an innocent man convicted of murder. After the truth was found out, he was prosecuted for malicious prosecution and stripped of his license to practice law.

Instead, if you want to persuade people, you should do all that has been discussed from the first chapter till now. I know it is hard work, but it pays at the end. Your kid gets to respect and appreciate you; your boss gives you that promotion, and your idea gets accepted, among other things. It is always better to seek to influence people rather than change the narrative to make them do your bidding.

CHAPTER EIGHT

Manipulation Isn't Influence

Desperation will make you want to achieve your objectives at all costs. It is the right attitude to have when you leave no stone unturned in your desire to get something done. Nonetheless, it is an issue when you don't mind hurting others to achieve your aim. One of the tools desperate people use to get what they want is manipulation.

Like I said earlier, it is not persuasion. It is more like a way of getting someone to do something for you to control the person. You will get what you want by fooling and manipulating them into doing it.

"Persuasion is the act of causing people to do or believe something"

Merriam Webster

This chapter will explore the ills of manipulative practices and how you can detect when such vices are used on you.

What Is Manipulation?

We can see the discrepancy even without going deep: manipulation controls someone to do something, and persuasion is making someone believe in something before they do it. Like I have explained in previous chapters before you can convince someone to do something, it must worth their time. However, manipulation, on the other hand, has to do with selfish interests. For instance, if you have watched the fresh prince of bel- air, there was a time Uncle Phil, Carlton, and Will went to a car dealer to get a car for Uncle Phil. Carlton tried to persuade Phil into buying the cheap and safe car, but Will cajoled him into buying a red, cool convertible.

He told him how lovely it would be if he drove the vehicle, how the bliss of youthful day would descend on him. He was deceived into buying the car. Meanwhile, Will only did it because he would get the chance to take it out with one of his dates. That is what deception looks like. It always has an underlying benefit that is driving the instigator.

On the other hand, persuasion convinces someone to go for something that you believe is in their best interest. In the example given above, Will would have encouraged his uncle if Phil had beforehand told will that he wanted a car that would make him feel younger again. The red convertible would have been the best option.

So, the fundamental discrepancy between the two is the intent with which you try to sway the person to do something. The purpose behind the former is the best interest of who you are getting to do something. However, the meaning behind the latter is what you stand to gain after the person had done that thing.

This has been corroborated by Nathaniel Nahai, who said that **both persuasive and manipulative approaches aim to influence people**, but the main difference between both is intent. According to Dr. Paul Swets, in his book, *The Art of Talking So That People Will Listen*, **"Manipulation aims at control, not cooperation. It results in a win/lose situation; It does not consider the good of the other party. Persuasion is just the opposite. In contrast to the controller, the persuader seeks to enhance the self-esteem of the other party. The result is that people respond better because they are treated as responsible, self-directing individuals."**

The definitions these two people have given us underline the difference between the two concepts. Yes, both seek to make people do something, but the intent to make people do those things is different. In a much simpler term, the first intends to hurt while the other endeavors to serve.

Persuaders find a way to use their knowledge and what they have acquired to the benefit of other people, while deceivers use their own experience for themselves. For instance, if someone walks up into a phone store and asks the guide for a product. The guide leads the customer through, giving him the specs and how each phone works. If he or she buys the phone, the guide has convinced the customer to buy the phone.

However, it is different if the boss had instructed the employees that whoever gets to sell a particular phone first would be given a promotion. If the guide showed the client only the phone the boss had said it would attract promotion, he or she has deceived the customer. However, this action can work against the company. Perhaps, the phone doesn't meet the requirements of what the client needed. That customer might feel cheated and not want to refer anyone to that store. He or she might also drop bad reviews on the company's website.

Also, I should add that gaining the undue advantage of others is not an excellent way of living, and it could also ruin businesses. Most perpetrators of this act don't have teams but people that work under them. They tend to have their customers leave without referrals, family with no love, and many more disadvantages.

Dark Manipulation

The two fundamental diversity of deception is white and dark. A white version is also a form that is of benefit to target. Indeed, I have said that control is orchestrated mainly for the benefit of the perpetrator. However, the white way is of more advantage to the target. Besides, it is not carried out with psychological violence, unlike the other diversity.

Psychological violence has to do with maiming people's mental innocence. It is an act orchestrated in forms of coercion, defamation, harassment, verbal insult, and many more actions that harm the psychological integrity of the victim. The government uses the white type to get the citizens to do something which would later be of great benefit to the citizens.

Parents also use it on small kids, which would deter them from hurting themselves. It is sometimes referred to as beneficial manipulation; it does not include emotional abuse, maltreatment, and intimate partner violence. However, for the scope of this discussion, we are going to be focusing more on diversity, which has to do with psychological violence.

Dark or grim-dark is said to be the most psychologically violating act of a perpetrator on a victim. It is divided into two: Dark psychology and Hypnosis. Dark manipulation involves getting people to do what they want for their sole benefit. Meanwhile, the white form is done out of altruism. Dark controllers use all forms of techniques, including lies, threat, coercion, harassment, defamation, blackmail, and many more, to get their targets to do what they want.

Dark Psychology

Dark psychology has to do with controlling the mind of your victims for you to get them to do your bidding. It is a straightforward tactic used by many people every day to achieve their aims, which are often malignant to the target. Most of the people in the world are selfish, with only a handful of altruism left. We all want to get what we cherish and which better way to get it than to make others get it for you? This is the psychology that is practiced by most of us in the world.

It is divided into three, namely: Narcissism, Machiavellianism, and Psychopathy, which are mainly referred to as Dark Triad. Narcissists are selfish, lack empathy, and grandiose in their vanity. These sets of people often use con arts to achieve their objectives by messing with their victim's heads. They don't give a hoot about what you feel as long as you understand what they want and carry it out.

Regarding Machiavellians, they have no sense of morals and use deceptive means to exploit others. They often cajole their victims into doing what they want. Psychopaths are more like narcissists. However, they will never show their actual color until they have achieved what they want from you. When you notice characteristics like selfishness, being very impulsive, lack of remorse and empathy, you are dealing with a psychopath.

These are the three sets of personalities that orchestrate dark arts. Indeed, you might do some of these things. However, that does not mean you belong to any of these categories. Nevertheless, it is not ideal for playing on the intelligence of others to accomplish your goals. If you realize that you have these traits, you need to rethink your actions or seek therapy when it is excessive.

Almost all of us have been victims or, at a point in our lives, practiced these arts to get what we want. For instance, when I was younger, during my teenage years, I often use these tactics to get my parents to give more freedom and autonomy, and most times, it worked. When talking about deception, we shouldn't forget to mention that most controllers are narcissistic. It means that they all are egoistic self-worshippers who care about nothing but themselves.

Narcissism And Dark Psychology

The most prevalent sets of persons that employ dark arts are those who are narcissistic. Narcissism is closely related to what was practiced under Adolf Hitler in the 1900s, which led to the first and second world wars. It was believed that a particular set of Europeans were unique and should be treated better than the rest. They tried to show their superiority, and when they were opposed, they resorted to violence. They wanted to rule the world, and they tried all they could to achieve their aim. Narcissistic individuals believe that they are unique and should get all they want. Therefore, they resolve into doing all they could to get it, and the most potent weapon in their arsenal is dark psychology.

How Narcissists Employ Dark Psychology

According to Perpetua Neo, narcissists have a culture of messing with people's minds. They do this to the extent that you have to do what they want. They use what Stephen Karpman calls the drama triangle, i.e., they play the rescuer, victim, and persecutor. They don't care how you feel and would make you do that which they want. The only thing that matters to them is the accomplishment of their selfish interests.

They are like a chameleon, and they shuffle between the drama triangle so easily and quickly that you don't know what to expect. In the words of Perpetua Neo, she described the experience with a narcissistic as walking on an eggshell, and you don't know what to anticipate. They would orchestrate perfectly all I have mentioned earlier. They put fear, guilt, or a sense of obligation into you, which makes you want to do what they want. Such individuals often start out by being nice to you. For example, they might get you a gift to make you feel obligated when they need your help.

They will stir up emotions in you by making you feel guilty if you don't do what they want. Such a person will remind you about his or her good deeds towards you. Then they will proceed into making you feel you are responsible for whatever they stand to lose from your refusal. Naturally, you don't want to be the reason anyone failed to achieve their targets. So, even when reluctant, you still help them accomplish their aims.

You may not feel the satisfaction of sacrificing for others when you help a narcissist. You are only doing what the person wants to avoid feeling bad about not helping out. If such a person is your spouse, you are in trouble because of your emotional attachment to him or her. He or she can tell you that you are turning him or her down because you are cheating with another person. You will want to prove that the person is wrong and end up doing what they want. It is not a palatable situation, but this is the reality of many individuals.

The Emotional Games Of A Narcissist

According to Psychology Today, narcissistic people believe that they are unique, and they would stop at nothing to attain the best, using people as a tool to achieve their goals. You should know that in their bid to gain attention, popularity, and what they want, they lie. Lying is one of the skills they are good at. They tell you various lies and try to deceive you into pitying them. They create in you a sense that they have suffered, and you would strive to be a good person to them and do all they want.

Naturally, you don't want anyone to suffer because of your inactions. So, you will want to help such persons out of compassion. However, you will be heartbroken when you realize that the person was only using you to achieve his or her aims. They tweak stories to make them look like victims earn your trust. Meanwhile, they have a grand plan, and you are nothing but a part of their emotional game. Winning at all costs is their trademark, and they can even murder to achieve their objectives.

You should also know that in a narcissistic person's overall scheme, they are overtly charming. They will make you feel special so that when it is your turn, you wouldn't be able to turn them down even though it is at your expense. Also, these people mainly dwell on insecurities. According to Bree Bonchay, they use third parties to help manipulate their victims. For instance, you don't want any other person, especially the opposite sex, to spend more time with your spouse than you. It is a natural sentiment we all have and will do anything to avoid.

Your partner can leverage that insecurity to make you spend more time with him or her. According to numerous studies, females often do this the most. They can tell their boyfriend that a colleague took them out for lunch just to make the guy do the same. When you refuse to do what they demand, they will start giving you the silent treatment. They stop talking to you to make you feel bad for not doing what they wanted you to do. They assume this power position and decide when and how to resume communication with you. When they do, they will make you feel guilty for the gap in the relationship they create by being selfish.

Hypnosis

The other form of dark manipulation is hypnosis. Most times, when you hear this word, you might imagine somebody snapping his fingers and using some kind of voodoo to make you act against your wish. You might picture a scenario where the person needs to ring a bell to lift the spell. I was in the same line of thought until I understood better when I started studying psychology. Hypnosis is not voodoo of any kind; it's just the usage of dark arts, which anybody can do. You might have done it before as well without knowing you were hypnotizing someone.

Hypnosis is a state a perpetrator puts you, which makes you feel relaxed and open to suggestions. The hypnotizer creates a vacuum in you where they can push in their mandate and make you do it for them. APA (American Psychological Association) has defined it as a state of consciousness involving focused attention and reduced peripheral awareness characterized by an enhanced capability for suggestions. This is what hypnosis is all about – suggestibility.

A person that hypnotizes another puts the person in a state of increased awareness, which makes them very accommodative to suggestions. That accommodation of new ideas is used by them to make you do what would be in their best interest. Meanwhile, the victim is not likely to accept that request on a norm. Jafar, a character in Aladdin (a Disney movie), comes to mind when you think about hypnosis. He uses a serpent staff to make the Sultan do whatever he wants until he was found out. Indeed, it is a form of hypnosis, but the procedure can be far less spiritual.

Hypnotic Power Words

There are certain words we use daily, which are hypnotic and control those we use them on. They are called hypnotic power words. Here they are:

Imagine

The first one, which is often used, is "**imagine**." This word takes your listeners away from the world of reality and puts them in a world where their fantasy would be fulfilled. You might not know it, but you have created in their hearts a kind of platform which would make them listen to your suggestion. Most people in business, salespeople, and other successful people use this word a lot.

For instance, there was a time I witnessed how a salesman made a woman buy a new washing machine. It was the same woman that was complaining about the hike in prices of products and how broke she was. When the salesman approached her, she waved him away, but he persisted, and he was finally able to gain her attention. The word that he used that even propelled me into wanting to buy the washing machine is "imagine."

He told the woman to imagine being in her house with a lot of dirty laundries and she was running late for work. By the time she is back from work, she would be exhausted. However, with a machine that was big enough to contain all the laundry and would dry them off itself, life would be more comfortable, without worries. The salesman put the woman into a trance in which she was able to see herself getting her laundry done immediately and effectively. She ended up buying it even after complaining about being low on cash.

Unequivocally, she wouldn't have bought it if he hadn't made her go into a trance where she could already see that her life was already more comfortable. Probably, she did laundry for her whole house and had kids. The product will improve her life. Nonetheless, it might not be her priority at that point. She might need to invest in other more pressing and urgent needs. However, he could convince her to make the washing machine number one in her scale of preference.

Also, there was a time my close friend used this technique to make me follow him for a date. I didn't want to follow him because I needed to do some more critical and urgent needs. However, he made me suspend those tasks to accompany him to an event that would not benefit me in any way. He met a lady he liked and wanted to go out with her, but she wouldn't go out with him alone. She wanted her friend to follow her.

He came to me and asked me to follow him, which I declined. He persisted and told me that I should imagine a lovely lady as the friend of the lady he was to be with. I was amazed by my imagination, and I decided to follow him. We got there, and the friend was pretty yeah, but she wasn't my type. The point is I wouldn't have followed my friend if he hadn't hypnotized me to follow him.

Because

Another hypnotic word we frequently use, which makes people do what we want or makes us do things for other people, is "**because**." According to J.F Kennedy, as humans, we crave order. We want to know why something was the way it was, what caused it to happen, and by so doing, we relate it to our personal lives. The word "because" is very hypnotic, and it makes people do what they wouldn't have necessarily done by stirring up our unconscious minds.

We hypnotize and get mesmerized by this word daily because we simply give a reason, regardless of whether it is a lie. When my friend told me that I should follow him, I was like, even if I was to follow him, what would be my benefit? He pointed this out by saying because going with him might help me get a girlfriend as well. It appealed to my hearing, and I decided to follow him. It is as simple as that. That's his curated hypnosis work.

A practical example has been given by Robert Cialdini when he used the response percent to illustrate how the word because it is hypnotic. He said that if you said: "Excuse me, can I use this machine because I am running late," you tend to get a 94% answer that would allow you to use it. However, if you say something like: "Excuse me, can I use the machine?" you'll get less than a 60% answer in the affirmative. This shows that this word is powerful enough to elicit responses from others. We use it every day without realizing its tremendous effects.

You

Another common word used that is hypnotic is "**You**." Have you ever wondered why adverts seem to be referring to you? Have you ever wondered why you think these big companies have you in mind? It's simple; they have deceived you into thinking it was you they were referring to. It is just simple hypnosis. They keep repeating the word "you," and before you know it, you are already ordering from their store with that money you saved for a vacation.

Hypnosis stimulates your imagination, paints pictures in your mind, link things that wouldn't usually go together, and distracts you. It activates your senses and creates associations that have never existed, and before you know it, you have done all that the hypnotist wants.

How Do You Know You Are Being Manipulated?

Many of us today get into things because we were manipulated into doing them, and we later regret doing those things. According to Sharie Stines, "**manipulation is an emotionally unhealthy psychological strategy used by people who are incapable of asking for what they want and need directly.**" Many people try to control each other at work, relationships, family, and different facets of life. However, before it goes too far, there are some signs that you will see, which would tell you that you are being influenced. Here they are:

Hypocrisy

The first thing you will notice about a controller is that what they say is quite different from how they behave. What do I mean? They would tell you what you want to hear, but they would end up doing another thing entirely.

There was a time in Eric's organization that they had to rise up and ask for a raise because they were being worked than how they were paid. Eric and his coworkers started the protest, which led to the destruction of some of the office equipment, but Eric's friend, who instituted the idea, was nowhere to be found.

When they were rounded up, he was sitting comfortably at his desk, going through his paperwork. He instigated them into protesting. Many of them had our contracts terminated because of him, and Eric still hold grudges against him. They make you think that what you were doing is right to fulfill their selfish interest.

This used them to gain a promotion for himself for being well-coordinated even during crisis. Meanwhile, he was the brain behind it. Immediately, someone starts acting in a way which is different from what they say, you should know that they are deceivers, and they would use you to achieve their selfish gains, and they wouldn't give a hoot for whatever later happens to you.

Pressure And Tension

Another thing that shows that you are being affected is that you feel fear, guilt, or an obligation to do it for them. Typically, you would not have felt this way about carrying out a task. Share Stines said that when someone is instigating you, you are psychologically coerced into doing something you don't want to do. You feel guilty for doing it, fear because you don't know what would happen if you don't do it or an obligation to do it.

According to Stines, there are two types of manipulators: the bullies and the victims. On the bully, you fear because he uses intimidation, threat, or aggression to get you to do things. You will always be apprehensive of what would happen if you refuse to do it so that you will obey. If you are going through this phase, you are being controlled. They would create a kind of trepidation in you that would galvanize you into action by using exaggeration to spur you into obedience.

Most lawyers and good sales associates are guilty of this. They would make their clients/customers think that if they don't do what they want them to do in time, there might be grave consequences. I had witnessed a situation when the clients of a lawyer didn't want to hire him because he was too expensive. He told them that they would spend more money looking for another lawyer, and before they do that, the opposition would have found favor in court. The clients were so scared that they had to settle down for his ridiculous fees.

On the part of the victim, you will feel guilty for not granting their request. Unlike bullies, they will not threaten you. However, you will still feel compelled to do their biddings. They will guilt trip you until you do it for them. My little nephew once used this tactic to make me grant his wish. He wanted an X-box, which I didn't plan on buying for him. The next time I went visiting, he cried because I didn't bring the X-box console I didn't promise him. That day, I took him to the store and got him an X-box 360, Something I wouldn't have done on a regular day. He made me buy it for him by crying, feigning that he was hurt because I didn't come along with his console.

According to Stine, the victim usually acts hurt... and the person who is targeted by the victim often tries to help the manipulator stop feeling guilty. In the instance of my nephew, I felt liable for making him cry, which was the primary reason I took him to the store to go and get the console.

Restructuring Reality

Also, another sign which shows that you are being deceived is that you start asking yourself questions about your reality. What do I mean by questioning your reality? According to Stines, con artists would twist what you have said and make it about themselves. They would make you feel you have done something wrong when, in reality, you haven't. Nonetheless, they would put it so correctly that you will end up questioning yourself.

They would tell you that what you have experienced is wrong, and they would say to you what happened in such a simple way that would make you think what happened is a figment of your imagination. Lawyers are learned experts in this field. They cook up stories while cross-examining the witness, manipulating the jury to discredit the testimony of the witness. There was one lawsuit I witnessed; It was a murder matter. The prosecuting attorney was cross-examining the accused's alibi. He said it was the alibi and the accused that committed the crime. He painted a convincing scenario that even the witness was second-guessing whether it was him telling the truth or the lawyer.

That is what they are like; they make you think that thing you have passed through isn't real, and it is their story that is right. You should also know that you might be in a relationship where the controller abuses the social norm of giving. For instance, it is natural for you to reciprocate when someone gives you a gift, in cash or kind. Stines call this "Mr. Nice Guy."

He gives you something, leaving a void in you, which would make you want to repay him. Whenever he wants something done, he calls on you, and you are ready to redeem yourself. If you don't heed to his calls, you will look ungrateful for the help he had rendered to you early. So, to every favor, gift, support, there's always a string attached. According to Stines, it is very confusing because you don't realize that something negative is going on, but with every good deed, gift, help, favor, there is a string attached."

"Exploiting the norms and expectations of reciprocity is one of the most common forms of manipulation."

Jay Olsen

According to Preston Ni, such an individual may insist on meeting you and interacting with you on a physical space to exert his dominance. So, if you want to know whether or not you are being controlled, you should find out how frequently you meet with your partner physically and if they exert dominance and control over you. If they do, you are in an unhealthy relationship.

What To Do When You Find Out You are Being Manipulated?

Many of us have received negative energy from people. However, they have controlled us for so long that we already think it is a norm. We don't know how to get out of the net of the controller. However, there are some ways you can go about getting the person to stop his or her antics. There are different approaches due to the various aspects of deception. The following tips will you in this regard.

Identify the Form

If you want to overcome being controlled by a "puppet master," you must know the type you are battling. You need to know whether the person is a victim or a bully. The easy way to do this is to notice when he person uses coercion or guilt to act against your wish. As earlier mentioned, the bully uses fear and threat while the victim uses guilt to hold you to ransom.

Establish Boundaries

One of the things you could do to overcome control is to establish boundaries. According to Stines, con artists have lousy limits. Since they are mostly narcissistic, they have limits that they would never make you cross because it might undermine their self-interest. However, they would want your attention all the time, jumping into your life and leaving anytime they want.

Be Patient

Another thing you could do when you are being controlled is that you should try the sleep on its tactic. If you are very impressed with something, you shouldn't just jump on it; you should find time to go through it and weigh the advantages over the consequences. A deceiver would want you right on any deal they have for you, but if you refrain yourself, you save yourself from being coerced into doing or buying something that you might later regret.

If you know that you are in a dangerous or unhealthy relationship, you can seek an expert's help on how to go about it. For instance, book a therapist. You will be given insight into what you have done wrong and how you can make it better. You can also try the more radical approach which, Stines termed "observe, don't absorb," which means that you shouldn't allow the behavior to affect you personally. She concluded with, "after all; we aren't responsible for anybody else's feeling." So, do not let anyone guilt-trip you into doing things against your wish because of their selfish antics.

The end... almost!

Reviews are not easy to come by.

As an independent author, I rely on readers, like you, to leave a short review on Amazon.

Even if it's just a sentence or two!

If you can't remember how to do it, don't worry, I'll guide you: just open "Returns & Orders", scroll down to find the book. On the right side you will find as last button "Write a review for the product".

So if you enjoyed the book, please...

I am very appreciative for your review as it truly makes a difference.

Thank you from the bottom of my heart for purchasing this book and reading it to the end.

Conclusion

The book has shown us how to persuade people. You would have realized by now that having the ability to do a job is not enough. Someone else can be given a role because he was more convincing in his presentation while you were hesitant. In an extremely competitive world, you need to leverage the finer details to stay relevant and be at the top of your game. In the same way, you might be ruining your relationship because of seemingly minute but critical details.

So far, we have been shown many ways in which we can win over others. Also, we have explored what we lacked that can make a person not want to listen to us and what we should apply to get the results we crave. Also, we have discussed what we could do that would get people to listen and what we want them to do but bring adverse repercussions later. We have explained how desperation might get you instant results but can backfire in the long run.

In the first chapter, we explicitly discussed how to get the right responses from our target audience. We were made to know that many people have the requisite qualities that others want, but they don't get enough people to get it from them because they don't know how to advertise themselves in the right way. In explaining how to promote ourselves in the best way, we got to know that we must be interested in know what others want.

Moreover, we learned that everybody in the world has needs, and you can only persuade someone to do what you want if it would satisfy any of their cravings. After knowing what the person wants, we must show them that what we want them to do would satisfy their wants. Another point is that it is not immediately that you convince people; it is a gradual process. So, you should not give up easily when things are not going your way. Sheer persistence can convince a pessimist to give you a chance to prove yourself.

The second chapter explicitly explains the reason why many people say no when we try to persuade them. The two methods of convincing others to do something are either with words or writing. That section dealt with why you get rejected when you try to persuade them by speaking to them. It was highlighted that there are numerous ways in which you talk, which turn people off from your proposal. It does not even matter how logically attractive it is.

Some of the reasons explained include: talking without confidence, using weasel words, which make our statements to lack conviction, among others. In writing, modes of writing, which turn people entirely off, were fully enumerated. The second chapter explained that we would never get the desired responses if we aren't empathetic enough. No one wants to trust someone they feel might have ulterior motives for asking them to commit to a project.

Just like chapter two, chapter three explained how people could persuade others in their speeches and in writing. How you could convince your listener is explained in depth using various examples of how big companies and brands win over prospective customers. Also, the third chapter gave an insight into how a person can write convincingly. We used examples of Steve Harvey and many other writers who have influenced people through what they have written down. Chapter three ended with what Kurt Mortensen has said about what can hinder successful persuasion.

Chapter four extensively talked about what body language is and why many people fail because they couldn't read the body language of their target audience. The importance of body language was enumerated, describing how it can be read. In chapter five, the importance of listening was discussed. We reiterated the fact that failing to listen is why many people struggle to succeed in various endeavors. Poor listening skills will affect your relationship with your loved ones and professional colleagues.

Most successful people speak less and listen more for them to know the right steps to take. For instance, it is through listening to a customer that someone would get to know what they want. Meanwhile, understanding the needs of the buyer is what enables you to satisfy the want. Also, things to stop doing to be a good listener are mentioned and explained explicitly in chapter five.

Chapter six majorly discussed how to be relevant in the political world. The tips in that chapter will enhance your political ambition. Examples of successful and significant political figures like Winston Churchill, Nelson Mandela, Dalai Lama, Abraham Lincoln won over people were cited. These would make you learn from those who have held political positions before. Their ability to cast a spell on their audience when speaking is noteworthy, and you can improve your speeches by emulating them.

In chapter seven, we are made to know that influence is about perception; that is, how you persuade people to do something depends on what you know or think about them. We were even made to understand that those that manipulate information also do it by altering the perception of their target audience. Meanwhile, chapter eight is on manipulation. The definition was given, and what makes it different from persuasion were highlighted. The primary difference is intent; because they both seek to influence people to do what something. For manipulation, the intent is the gain of the manipulator, while persuasion focuses on the target.

In chapter eight, how to know that someone is being controlled was explained. Tips on what to do when someone knows they are being manipulated were also presented. Also, the two main types of manipulation are stated: white and dark. White manipulation is not well discussed because it doesn't cause any psychological violence. This type can be to the benefit of the target. Those in government offices often leverage it to keep the sanity of society.

However, dark manipulation was explored in detail because it is orchestrated by inflicting psychological violence. The two modes in which dark manipulation is carried out were enumerated: dark psychology and hypnosis. From the explanation and the explicit examples that have been given, you should be able to win over anyone with ease without manipulating them.

References

www.robert-reed.org

https://blog.hubspot.com/sales/weasel-words-sales-conversations

https://www.quickanddirtytips.com/education/writing/avoid-these-4-common-persuasive-writing-mistakes

https://www.tpsnva.org/teach/lq/016/persinstr.pdf

https://www.skillsyouneed.com/ips/empathy.html

https://copyblogger.com/persuasive-copywriting-words/

https://www.skillsyouneed.com/ips/barriers-communication.html

https://www.tpsnva.org/teach/lq/016/persinstr.pdf

https://www.skillsyouneed.com/ips/persuasion-skills.htmlhttps://www.skillsyouneed.com/ips/negotiation-persuasion-skills.html

https://www.skillsyouneed.com/ips/questioning.htmlhttps://www.skillsyouneed.com/ips/question-types.html

https://www.skillsyouneed.com/ips/ineffective-listening.html

https://www.skillsyouneed.com/ips/what-is-communication.html

https://www.skillsyouneed.com/ips/ineffective-listening.html

https://www.skillsyouneed.com/ips/listening-principles.htmlhttps://www.skillsyouneed.com/ips/listening-types.html

https://www.skillsyouneed.com/ips/active-listening.html

https://www.skillsyouneed.com/ips/feedback.html

http://content.time.com/time/specials/packages/completelist/0,29569,2046285,00.html

http://content.time.com/time/specials/packages/article/0,28804,2046285_2045996_2046135,00.html

http://content.time.com/time/specials/packages/article/0,28804,2046285_2045996_2046090,00.html

http://content.time.com/time/specials/packages/article/0,28804,2046285_2045996_2045851,00.html

http://content.time.com/time/specials/packages/article/0,28804,2046285_2045996_2046001,00.html

http://content.time.com/time/specials/packages/article/0,28804,2046285_2045996_2045990,00.html

https://www.demilked.com/faking-luxury-lifestyle-byron-denton/http://content.time.com/time/specials/packages/article/0,28804,2046285_2045996_2045990,00.htmlhttps://michaelwroberts.com/content/persuasion-manipulation/#:~:text=Persuasion%20isn%27t%20evil.&text=But%2C%20the%20person%20you%27re,as%20to%20serve%20one%27s%20purpose."

https://time.com/5411624/how-to-tell-if-being-manipulated/https://www.healthline.com/health/mental-health/emotional-manipulation#excessive-sharing

https://www.psychologytoday.com/us/blog/communication-success/201903/7-ways-narcissists-manipulate-relationships#:~:text=The%20narcissist%20may%20regularly%20use,others%20into%20surrendering%20their%20boundaries.

https://www.psychologytoday.com/us/blog/lifetime-connections/201911/three-ways-narcissists-manipulate-their-partners

https://medium.com/@FlexMR/research-ethics-differentiating-manipulation-from-persuasion-3c53bea8d5e9

https://medium.com/@FlexMR/research-ethics-differentiating-manipulation-from-persuasion-3c53bea8d5e9

https://www.jonathanfields.com/the-line-between-persuasion-and-manipulation/

https://www.talentsmart.com/articles/9-Signs-You're-Dealing-With-an-Emotional-Manipulator-2147446691-p-1.html

https://michaelwroberts.com/content/persuasion-manipulation/#:~:text=Persuasion%20isn%27t%20evil.&text=But%2C%20the%20person%20you%27re,as%20to%20serve%20one%27s%20purpose

http://kparedes91.blogspot.com/2008/03/persuasive-speech-gettysburg-address-by.html?m=1

https://hbr.org/2015/04/why-the-gettysburg-address-is-still-a-great-case-study-in-persuasion

https://www.duarte.com/learn-to-communicate-from-nelson-mandela-a-communicator-who-cares/

https://www.theguardian.com/world/2013/dec/07/nelson-mandela-freedom-fighter-john-carlin

https://www.secondnature.com.au/blog/how-winston-churchill-presented-his-speeches-to-inspire/

https://www.successconsciousness.com/blog/personal-development/the-benefits-of-being-a-good-listener/

https://www.inc.com/minda-zetlin/7-reasons-why-its-smart-to-listen-more-than-you-talk.html

https://hypnosistrainingacademy.com/3-surefire-power-words-to-gain-power-and-influence-people-fast/

https://neilpatel.com/blog/3-hypnotic-power-words/

http://drjasonjones.com/dark_psychology/

https://time.com/5380312/is-hypnosis-real-science/

www.ingramcontent.com/pod-product-compliance
Lightning Source LLC
Chambersburg PA
CBHW070345220526
45467CB00001B/251